A Dad's Guide
to Praying
for His
Kids

Steve Chapman

HARVEST HOUSE PUBLISHERS
EUGENE, OREGON

A DAD'S GUIDE TO PRAYING FOR HIS KIDS
Copyright © 2016 by Steve Chapman
Published by Harvest House Publishers
Eugene, Oregon 97402
www.harvesthousepublishers.com

ISBN 978-0-7369-5591-1 (pbk.)
ISBN 978-0-7369-5592-8 (eBook)

Library of Congress Cataloging-in-Publication Data
    Names: Chapman, Steve.
    Title: A dad's guide to praying for his kids / Steve Chapman.
    Other titles: Wednesday's Prayer
    Description: Eugene, Oregon : Harvest House Publishers, 2016. | Rev. ed. of: Wednesday's Prayer. 1998.
    Identifiers: LCCN 2015021778 | ISBN 9780736955911 (pbk.)
    Subjects: LCSH: Fathers—Religious life. | Intercessory prayer—Christianity
    Classification: LCC BV4529.17 .C44 2016 | DDC 248.8/421—dc23 LC record available at http://lccn.loc.gov/2015021778

Printed in the United States of America

16 17 18 19 20 21 22 23 24 / VP-JC / 10 9 8 7 6 5 4 3 2 1

To my beloved children,
Nathan and Heidi, and their spouses and their children,
for whom I gladly pray.

Wednesday's Prayer

Father God, to You I come
In the name of Your Son
I bring my children to Your throne
Father, hear my cry

Above all else, Lord, save their souls
Draw them near You; keep them close
Be the shield against their foes
Make them Yours, not mine

Give them peace in Christ alone
In their sorrow, be their song
No other joy would last as long
Father, calm their fears

Guide their feet, Lord; light their path
May their eyes on You be cast
Give their hands a kingdom task
A purpose for their years

And as my flesh cries out for bread
May I hunger, Lord, instead
That my children would be fed
On Your words of life

So, Father God, to You I come
In the name of Your Son
I bring my children to Your throne
Father, hear my cry[1]

Contents

The Rewarding Journey Ahead   7

1. The Heritage of Prayer   12

2. Digging In   18

3. The First Steps   21

4. What Is Effective Praying?   30

5. Why Fast?   33

6. What Is Fasting?   36

7. What Fasting Is Not   43

8. The Advantages of Fasting   50

9. The Vestal Intervention   55

10. Guidelines for Fasting   65

11. When to Pray   76

12. What to Pray   82

A Good Framework for Praying for Your Children

13. "Father God, to You I Come"   91

14. "In the Name of Your Son"   94

15. "I Bring My Children to Your Throne"   96

16. "Father, Hear My Cry"   99

17. "Above All Else, Lord, Save Their Souls"   101

18. "Draw Them Near You; Keep Them Close"   103

19. "Be the Shield Against Their Foes"   106

20. "Make Them Yours, Not Mine" 109

21. "Give Them Peace in Christ Alone" 111

22. "In Their Sorrow, Be Their Song" 113

23. "No Other Joy Would Last as Long" 116

24. "Father, Calm Their Fear" 119

25. "Guide Their Feet, Lord; Light Their Path" 122

26. "May Their Eyes on You Be Cast" 124

27. "Give Their Hands a Kingdom Task,
    a Purpose for Their Years" 126

28. "As My Flesh Cries Out for Bread,
    May I Hunger, Lord, Instead" 128

29. "[I Pray] That My Children Would
    Be Fed on Your Words of Life" 129

30. What to Do Thursday to Tuesday 131

31. Wear the Prayer 135

32. Write a Note 137

    Your Child Is Not Out of Reach 138

    Notes 143

The Rewarding Journey Ahead

The evening was to be an enjoyable time of reconnecting with friends at a local restaurant. When we gathered with them in the waiting area, my wife, Annie, and I knew immediately that something wasn't right. There was a noticeable tension between the other couple as we all talked. As our time together began to fade, the urgency we felt about asking if things were okay with them bore down on us. Finally, Annie spoke up.

"How are you two doing?"

Her question forced the door open to some serious conversation that lasted nearly until closing time. Annie and I tipped the waiter very well for the extra time we spent in the booth with our precious but hurting friends. We discovered that their teenaged daughter was the source of their current struggles. Her rebellious behavior and choosing to associate with some young people who had very questionable moral standards caused the two of them to feel their child was slipping away into the abyss of hopelessness.

Annie, who is incredibly perceptive, asked, "How is this affecting the two of you?"

The wife responded with an alarming answer. "We can't stand each other. Every time we look at one another, we see only blame for the condition our daughter is in. Something has to change; otherwise, our family is going to completely fall apart."

Our hearts were moved by their desperate cry for comfort and encouragement. We knew their marriage had to be first on the list of things that needed attention, and rightly so. As we talked, they agreed to make it a priority to seek counseling regarding their relationship. But as much as their marriage needed help, I felt a gnawing need to address their daughter's situation as well.

The Reclamation Plan

The dad was at a loss about how to reach his firstborn. Too many arrivals back home after midnight and far too many of her friends leading her into unacceptable types of entertainment had sapped his strength and willingness to think about his wife.

With the knowledge that his girl was on a course too dangerous to ignore, I felt compelled to suggest to my friend that the two of us go to God on his daughter's behalf. "Let's begin praying in earnest for your daughter," I said. "And to show God that we're serious about this, I'm willing to fast a full day at least once a week with you on her behalf." Little did I know that just a few days prior, the Lord had impressed on his heart to add fasting to his prayers for his child. Though he'd never faced that type of challenge, he was confident God was leading him to do so.

Without hesitation, he enthusiastically responded. "Let's do it. I really want to see God do a mighty work in my girl."

His wife sort of laughed at the idea of us fasting for all our kids. I don't believe her reaction to our plan was malicious. I'm convinced that it indicated just how hopeless she was feeling too.

In spite of her doubt, her husband and I set out to reclaim their teenager. That night the dad and I agreed that Wednesdays seemed to be the best day for both of us. It was midweek and a church night, as well as the least busy day in both our work schedules. Thus began a journey for the two of us that lasted a couple of years.

How grateful I am to report that the daughter made a spiritual one-eighty. It didn't happen in an instant, but like a big ship turning around, the teenager slowly began to show signs of moving toward the Lord. Gradually her friend base changed, and the influence of godly young people replaced the bad company that had helped corrupt her morals. Her late-night escapades ceased, and she became more accountable in terms of her whereabouts. Today, she is a totally different person.

One of the sweetest moments I've ever experienced in a church service was on an Easter Sunday about three years after my friend and I started "doing Wednesdays" together. Annie and I had taken seats in the balcony of the church. As worship music filled the room, Annie nudged me and quietly pointed toward our friends sitting below us on the main floor. What I saw filled my heart with indescribable joy. Standing next to her dad was the daughter who had been the subject of our prayers on Wednesdays. The memory of the hunger pangs that accompanied the fasting disappeared as I saw her lift her hands in praise to our Father in heaven. God had heard our cries and answered our prayers. What a beautiful sight!

Admittedly, the years of prayer were an emotional roller coaster ride as her dad and I invested time in our quest for her soul's salvation and redemption. We had to face some hard facts, including:

- The daughter, like all the rest of us, was born with a sinful nature, and because of it, she was prone to sin (Romans 3:23; 7:18).

- Satan was ready at all times to target her weaknesses just "as the serpent deceived Eve by his craftiness" (2 Corinthians 11:3).

Ultimately, we realized that our struggle wasn't against her flesh and blood, but against the unseen forces that sought to deceive her (Ephesians 6:12). Yet our confidence in the Lord's ability to overcome Satan, the "god of this world," remained strong.

The accountability my friend and I set up was a key to keeping our commitment to the regimen of prayer and fasting. We regularly checked up on each other and our self-imposed prayer schedule when we met in church or in the woods while hunting. Not much was said other than, "Still doin' Wednesdays?" The answer was never long. Normally it was just a smile and a determined, "Yep!"

What seemed to encourage us the most was seeing the little changes in the daughter's life or hearing a sweet word that she hadn't said in a long while. These indications that she was coming home to Christ spurred us on. Watching God at work was a spiritual delight. Add to that the dad's absolute and unconditional love for his teenager, and the unfolding miracle was glorious.

Though the outcome has been extremely gratifying to us both, we've agreed that it is more important now than ever before that we continue in our prayers and fasting for all our kids...and now our grandkids. Satan doesn't cease in his pursuit of our children, and neither should we let up in the battle. So the "Wednesday's Prayer" continues on. We will, hopefully, persist until our last day on earth.

What about you? In your role as parent, is this the time you want to get serious in your prayers for your kids? Maybe your child is:

- yet to be born
- a babe in your arms
- a toddler
- an adolescent
- a teenager
- a college student
- grown and out of the nest
- raising their own children

At whatever stage of parenting you might be in, if you're concerned about the spiritual health and eternal destination of your children and want to establish a regimen of prayer and fasting for them, this book will help you.

A Dad's Guide to Praying for His Kids is a quick read designed to jump-start the rewarding journey you're setting out on. As you hold your ground against the enemy, I encourage you to draw on the knowledge that God is more than willing to hear you and to intervene on behalf of your children and your grandchildren:

> I love the LORD because He hears my voice and my supplications. Because He has inclined His ear to me, therefore I shall call upon Him as long as I live (Psalm 116:1-2).

1

The Heritage of Prayer

Because my mom and dad were followers of Christ when I was born to them in 1950, my memories of growing up include images of them praying regularly. Though my sister and I knew them as Christians, their salvation experience didn't take place until after they married in 1947—well, actually, just after my sister was born in 1949.

My mother was a good mom, but before my sister and I came along she admittedly lived apart from God. Her independent attitude regarding the Lord was drastically changed when she was introduced to Christianity and accepted Jesus at a local revival being held at a church near the town of Chapmanville, West Virginia. I'll let her tell you about her experience in her own words:

> I had decided to start going to night classes in Logan, WV, to learn nursing so I could get a job outside of our home. I hadn't been going to school but a little while, when one evening as I walked out of the hollow where we lived toward the main highway to catch the bus to town, I heard music coming from a church up on the hill. The sound somehow touched my soul and drew me in.
>
> I decided to abandon my trip to Logan for night school and headed up the hill to the church building. That night I heard the preaching of the gospel message. By the end of the preacher's sermon I had no doubt that I was spiritually lost and knew I had

to respond when the invitation was given. I felt compelled to go forward and kneel at the altar. That was the night I gave my life to Christ. The amount of fear I felt in knowing that I was not right with God was tremendous, but I felt a far greater joy and peace when I realized I had made the choice to ask Him to forgive me of my sins and fill my heart.

After the lengthy service at the church I headed home where P.J., my husband, was taking care of our baby. When I walked in the house he said, "How was school?" I put my shoulders back and answered, "I don't know. I didn't go. I went to a revival instead...and I got saved tonight!"

My sweet husband was bewildered by my choice but didn't challenge it. In fact, he agreed to go with me two nights later. And when he did, he heard the gospel and also responded to the call to go to the altar. That night he surrendered his life to the Lord.

Family history says that the change in my parents' lives was so extensive that it was no exaggeration to say that from that revival meeting on, each time the doors of the church were opened they were walking through them. After I was born, they took my sister and me along. They made sure that all four us were faithful attendees. Eventually, dad responded to a call on his life to become a preacher. On a bi-vocational basis, he took a pastor's position in the town of Point Pleasant, West Virginia.

By the time my sister and I reached our teen years, we were well engrained in church, not only through our dad's role as minister but also, especially, in the music department. My sister had become quite the singer, and my mother taught me to play the acoustic guitar. I started learning piano as well. On the keyboard, I enjoyed mimicking the piano style of the late, great country-style pianist Floyd Cramer. With his influence and some self-training, I developed enough skill at the ivories to play during the services. (I was known to occasionally render one of his popular songs, "Last Date," during altar services…at least until my mother recognized the melody.)

My participation, as well as my sister's, in my parents' work at the church gave them great satisfaction. They were thrilled to be working as a foursome and seeing great results from their labor in the form of new converts and a growing number of attendees in the pews. Of course, the devil doesn't like that kind of progress for God's kingdom. One of the ways he tried to thwart it was to go after the preacher's son…me. Unfortunately, I fell for and then participated in the enemy's plot.

In my early teens I began to slide down the slippery slope of worldly enticements. I lost interest in being part of the church. Secular music (especially the groups that filtered over from Britain) and non-Christian friends at school were major influences that attracted me. My folks could easily see that their son's heart was being led away from the fold. Add to that the typical angst that seems to accompany the teen years, and my parents had a significant battle on their hands.

It was in that era of time that my mother shocked me one morning with a prayer I will never forget. I was lying in bed around eight o'clock in the morning. I was used to the smell of breakfast when I woke up; however, I didn't detect the aroma of bacon and biscuits this day. I didn't know that my mother was still in her bedroom talking to God about me. With righteous exasperation, she came bursting into mine.

As I attempted to rouse myself from a sleepy stupor, she dropped to her knees at my bedside, grabbed my forearm with both hands, and abruptly and earnestly started praying. The words I heard as she spoke tearfully to God are in the chorus of the following song

I wrote about the incident a few years later. I affectionately call it "Mama's Brave Prayer."

To help you understand how uneasy her unexpected cry to God made me feel, you need to keep in mind that I had watched God answer my mother's prayers often and sometimes within minutes. She had a connection with God that was remarkable and also very intimidating. And this sweet, humble woman I called my dear mama prayed this powerful prayer over me.

Mama's Brave Prayer

One day in my early teenage years
Mama came into my room with tears
She said, "I've put it off too long
What I've got to do seems wrong..."
Next to my bed she fell on her knees
She laid her hard-working hands on me
Looked up to Jesus and told Him she cared
That's when I heard my mama's brave prayer

"If you see he'll die a sinner
If you see he'll trade the right for the wrong
Then all I ask of you, sweet Jesus,
Go ahead, right now, and take him on home!"

She said, "Amen," and the room grew still
I'll not forget the fear I could feel
And the moments passed
So have the years
I'm glad to say that I'm still here

Now looking back I can see it's true
She loved my flesh and my spirit too
Now heaven waits us, and I believe I'll be there
I'll be forever grateful for my mama's brave prayer

"If you see he'll die a sinner
If you see he'll trade the right for the wrong
Then all I ask of you, sweet Jesus,
Go ahead, right now, and take him on home!"[2]

Needless to say, that was the morning I first learned what cold sweat was all about. I honestly thought my life was going to come to a screeching halt after my mother finished her very courageous prayer. Like the lyric says, "I'm glad I'm still here!"

Why Such an Aggressive Approach?

So why would anyone offer a prayer like my mother's? My answer is that my mom prayed such an aggressive prayer because she knew the worst thing that could ever happen to one of her children was not that they would flunk out of school, marry a jerk, or even fall prey to a deadly disease. While those things are indeed awful and definitely undesirable, she believed the absolute worst thing that could ever befall her kids is that they would die without Christ in their hearts. She was convinced that the result of such a tragedy would be that her children would suffer the consequences of the eternal, unquenchable flames of hell, forever separated from God and those who love them (Mark 9:48). As she put it, "If that's not enough reason for any mom and dad to pray for their child, I don't know what is!"

Based on my experience with the relentless prayers of my parents for me, I say to all of us dads (and moms) that one of the major contributors to our children's spiritual health is when we engage in serious and persistent prayers that our children will accept Christ, know His salvation, and walk in His ways throughout their life-times. It's only because of Christ's intervention in their lives that they will know the kind of joy the Bible calls "inexpressible and full of glory" (1 Peter 1:8) And someday, when time is no more, as a result of God's work in our children, we can be with them in heaven rejoicing around His throne and celebrating the everlast-ing peace and safety that are found only in His eternal presence.

Are you praying in earnest for your children? If so, may God bless your prayers. Are you wondering if there's more you can do? The answer is yes! Please keep reading.

2

Digging In

It's likely that at some time in your life you've slowly driven by a serious car wreck on the highway and felt that squeamish feeling that accompanies the sight. Do you remember how the emotions stayed with you, haunted you, and caused you to drive very carefully for the next several miles? Then at some point down the road, the memory of the tragedy faded and gradually the needle on the RPM gauge on your dash climbed upward again.

What I just described is a very good picture of my teen years after my mama's brave prayer. Her very bold show of love gripped my heart for a long time. Then, as I entered my late teens and journeyed on into my twenties, enough years had gone by that I felt comfortable putting aside godly fear. That's when I pushed the "pleasure pedal" and intentionally sped toward the sins that had been forbidden in my youth.

By then I'd decided to postpone college and, feeling adventurous, I joined the Navy. Unlike my time at the nearby university I was attending that kept me physically close to my family and friends, when I headed off to faraway places in the military, I found myself practically alone when it came to companionship.

As a sailor, I was moved around to the naval bases in the big cities of Chicago, Memphis, and Norfolk. In these places, out of eyesight of those who loved me and held me accountable to good moral standards, I chose to "carry out the desires of the flesh" (Galatians 5:16). The well-known quip "Character is who you are when there ain't nobody lookin'" contains a truth that I mocked during my military days. I was entering what I now call my dark ages.

While it was sadly true that the enemy of my soul had escalated his battle tactics that were aimed at my destruction, my folks had also kicked into high gear in terms of their prayerful determination to see their kids in heaven. They were very familiar with the words in 1 Peter 5:8: "Be of sober spirit, be on the alert. Your adversary, the devil, prowls around like a roaring lion, seeking someone to devour." Mom and Dad were not about to let the enemy win or intimidate them with his growls. Their hunger to see their son return to the safety of a walk with Christ consumed them.

The Hunger Tactic

My folks embraced 2 Corinthians 10:3-4 as absolute truth. The verses say, "Though we walk in the flesh, we do not war according to the flesh, for the weapons of our warfare are not of the flesh, but divinely powerful for the destruction of fortresses." They knew that the fight would be won only with God's help. So they turned to the Lord and poured their hearts into praying for me. As a result, they willingly became very acquainted with self-imposed hunger—a sacrifice that is challenging for sure.

My parents also received inspiration to add fasting to their prayers from the account in Matthew 17:14-21 that tells about a man going to Jesus and falling on his knees asking Him to have mercy on his son. The dad said, "He is a lunatic and is very ill; for he often falls into the fire and often into the water." The desperate dad proceeded to tell Jesus, "I brought him to Your disciples, and they could not cure him."

Jesus spoke to the disciples saying, "You unbelieving and perverted generation, how long shall I be with you? How long shall I put up with you? Bring [the son] to Me."

They brought the son to Jesus. He rebuked him, a demon came out of him, and he was immediately cured. Seeing the miracle, the disciples asked Jesus, "Why could we not drive it out?" The answer Jesus gave represented a major challenge for his disciples:

> Because of the littleness of your faith; for truly I say to you, if you have faith the size of a mustard seed, you will say to this mountain, "Move from here to there," and it will move; and nothing will be impossible to you. But this kind does not go out except by prayer and fasting (verses 20-21).

Taking Christ's words at face value and believing God would honor their choice to forego food for the sake of showing Him how intensely serious they were about their son, my folks began to skip meals and pray. While they didn't put me in the category of a lunatic, they were well aware that I was spiritually falling often into the fires of sin and into the waters of unholy pleasure.

All the while, as I fed my appetite for what the world had to offer in terms of fleshly indulgences, my parents were digging trenches in the battlefield where they fought for my eternal life. I had no idea that I was being so hotly pursued, but blessed be the name of the Lord for seeing to it that I was in the sights of my parents' loaded weapons of prayer and fasting.

God, in His great mercy and kindness, eventually answered my parents' aggressive praying, but before I tell you how and when He did, I want to first address these questions in the chapters that follow:

- What is the first step to take toward using prayer as a way to reach your children?
- What is meant by "effective praying"?
- Why fast?
- What is fasting?
- What is fasting not?
- What are the advantages of fasting?

3

The First Steps

"I have no greater joy than this, to hear of my children walking in the truth." These words found in 3 John 4, referred to spiritual children, but when applied to the role of the parent, the sentiment is the same.

If it's true that a parent feels great joy in knowing that a child is choosing to walk in the truths of Christ, it stands to reason that great sorrow would come from seeing a child refuse to follow Him. When I read the well-known account of the prodigal son, I imagine what anguish his father must have felt when he thought of his wayward child (Luke 15). I envision him standing and looking down the road, wishing with all his broken heart that he would see his son walking back home. I picture the dad crying in anguish as wave after wave of sadness washes against the shores of his heart.

The story of the prodigal is heart-wrenching indeed, but how wonderful to know it ends with the son returning home to a joyful reception. He was incredibly blessed to have been on the receiving end of such a boundless measure of his father's love. Because I too was a prodigal, someday when I get to heaven I want to meet that son and, together, we will give thanks to God for having been shown such an abundance of unconditional love.

Urgency of the Emergency

We're not told in the biblical account of the prodigal if the father aggressively prayed for his son's repentant return, but I tend to think he did. I draw this conclusion based on how intensely I know my folks prayed for me. It's as though they created their own spiritual branch of the military called "The Prayer Force" as they daily sent their petitions skyward to heaven.

While they did indeed exert some aggressive prayers, my parents admitted that it wasn't until they felt alarm at the very thought that I would be a lost soul forever that they sensed the "urgency of the emergency." It was the rush of overwhelming concern for me that contributed to their willingness to go to war with their prayer guns blazing. I refer to the state of heart they entered into as "battletude."

Sadly, however, too many fathers and mothers of lost children haven't yet awakened to the reality of their children's need for a Savior. For some, the reason this is true is they don't realize their own need for salvation, which is *the first step* to leading their children to their heavenly home with Jesus. Only God knows what it will take to bring unaware parents to the realization of their personal need for His redemption. Though it is disheartening to see so many moms and dads who are oblivious to the extent of the emergency, it's always encouraging to hear about those who do wake up to it. Such was the case for a dad I heard about whose eyes were opened to his need for salvation by something his son said one morning at breakfast. This true story is told in this song lyric.

I Want to Go with My Daddy

> He hid behind his Sunday-morning paper
> His little boy behind a box of Cheerios
> She poured some coffee and thought about the church
> Where their family never goes
>
> When she brought it up, he said, "I won't be going.
> I guess I'm headed to that place made for sinners like me."
> Then she asked their little boy across the table,
> "Would you like to go to church with me?"
> And he said...

"I want to go with my daddy
To that place he said is made for him,
    that's what I want to do
'Cause I love my daddy,
    and wherever he's going
I want to go there too."

He never had any words cut him deeper
And he couldn't hide the tears on his face
She said, "If we hurry we can make it!"
He had a change of destination on that day
'Cause he heard...

"I want to go with my daddy
To that place he said is made for him,
    that's what I want to do
'Cause I love my daddy and
    wherever he's going
I want to go there too."

Now they can sing "Amazing Grace" together
And he can smile when he hears his little boy say...

"I want to go with my daddy
To that place he said is made for him,
    that's what I want to do
'Cause I love my daddy and
    wherever he's going
I want to go there too."[4]

The uncle of the young dad featured in the song lyric shared this inspiring story with me. He beamed as he reported that the little family was doing well, and the dad was especially grateful to have been alerted to his need for spiritual redemption by what his little boy said. He came to grips with the sobering fact that, like it or not, he was a strong influence in his son's heart.

If the story about the father who realized he needed to have "a change of destination" is one that speaks to you about your own need to do the same, why wait to make the turn to Him when you can do it right now? If you want to make that life-changing decision, I invite you at this moment to pray the following prayer. As you read it (aloud if the setting allows), you can trust that God will hear you because of the comforting words found in Isaiah 55:6-7: "Seek the LORD while He may be found; call upon Him while He is near. Let the wicked forsake his way and the unrighteous man his thoughts; and let him return to the LORD, and He will have compassion on him, and to our God, for He will abundantly pardon." With that gracious and trustworthy promise in mind, this prayer will help you begin walking with Christ:

> God, I come to You and acknowledge that I am a sinner in need of the salvation You offer through Your Son, Jesus Christ. I accept as truth the good news that He shed His blood on the cross of Calvary and died for my sins. I believe Jesus was buried and on the third day He rose from the dead and the resurrected life He claimed is now mine. I receive it by grace through faith in Your Son alone and confess that salvation comes not through anything I've done or could ever do but by what You have done for me through Your Son. Thank You for forgiveness. I ask You to transform my life and help me follow Your Son and Your Word all the rest of my days. In the name of Your Son, Jesus Christ, I ask this.

If you chose to pray this prayer, I welcome you to the family of Christ followers! There's much to learn, but for starters I encourage you to begin meeting with other believers at a local, Bible-based church. Read and study the Bible. I also urge you to publically let others know about this decision you've made by getting baptized (Matthew 3:11; John 3:4-17; Acts 8:30-39). May God bless you and keep you in His care as you begin this marvelous journey and as you lead others to Him—especially your children.

The Next Step

Whether you just yielded your life to Christ or have been following Him for a while, when it comes to your children the urgency regarding their spiritual destination demands taking yet another very important step. Simply stated, to help a child live righteously, we ourselves must live righteously. To assist you in understanding the importance of this truth, I offer an illustration that I included in my book *A Look at Life from a Deer Stand Devotional.*

> All who have been on a commercial airliner know that when we get aboard and they close the door, what follows is the safety speech that is delivered by the flight attendants to the passengers. Part of their verbiage includes the familiar warning about the emergency oxygen mask. It goes something like this:
>
> > In the unlikely event of a loss of cabin pressure, a mask will fall out of the ceiling above you. Take the mask and place it over your nose and mouth and breathe normally.
> >
> > If you have someone sitting next to you who needs assistance, put the mask on yourself first before assisting them." [Is hyperventilating "normal"?]
>
> The reason for the last part of the flight attendant's instructions is obvious to most of us. If we pass out because we don't first tend to our own need for breathable air, we'll be of no use to the person who needs our

help. Without realizing it, every time flight attendants deliver their safety speech, they're preaching the truth found in Psalm 51, which includes David's contrite prayer of repentance for his sin with Bathsheba. He prays, "Wash me thoroughly from my iniquity...wash me, and I shall be whiter than snow...blot out all of my iniquities. Create in me a clean heart...Do not cast me away from Your presence and do not take Your Holy Spirit from me. Restore to me the joy of Your salvation..."

The elements of David's prayer are almost painful to read. Can't you feel the contrition in his soul? But after he gets it right with God, he starts verse 13 with a statement that is especially applicable to parenting. The psalmist says, "*Then* I will teach transgressors Your ways."

It seems that David was very aware that he would have no right to guide anyone else if he himself didn't first repent of his great errors and experience a revival of his pursuit of righteousness. What an example he set to follow.

May God give each of us who are aware of our spiritual shortcomings the courage to pray verses one through twelve of Psalm 51 *before* we apply the words of verse thirteen. Our children need us to first be qualified with a life of holiness before we *then* teach them [our little transgressors] His ways.

Be on the Alert

Unfortunately, far too many dads and moms have yet to realize their homes are like damaged airplanes that are, spiritually speaking, spiraling out of the sky. They are oblivious to how Satan has slithered into their lives and, ultimately, into the hearts of their children. They can't see that he is a venomous viper who is clever enough to know that going through the front door of a home would be too noticeable. Instead, he looks for less obvious ways to slip into the life of a family. Very often he'll find a crack in the wall of the home caused by a parent accepting something they believe isn't all that harmful but really is. An example of that type of opening might be the entertainment a mom and dad allows and endorses. Permitting a steady diet of brain-numbing nonsense that comes through network television, cable channels, low-standard movies, and unwholesome books and magazines can chisel away at the hearts of the members of a family.

I believe that most of what is produced in Hollywood isn't just a source of entertainment. The products are also designed to reshape and remold the minds and hearts of audiences. And so often what we parents consider mild and acceptable in terms of content is ultimately the bait used by the destroyer to entice our kids into the trap of more sordid and immoral material. One wise observer noted, "What parents accept in moderation, the children will embrace in excess."[5] That's a sobering thought, but very true.

Far worse than what the whole family might devour in terms of worthless entertainment is what some parents might consume in secret. In many cases, they do so with the foolish assumption that it affects no one else, including their kids. To the contrary, whatever a mom or dad does, whether openly or in secret, will eventually have an effect in the lives of their children. Consider this truth in Lamentations 5:7: "Our fathers sinned, and are no more; it is we who have borne their iniquities."

It is an undeniable reality that a parent's transgressions will have a negative effect on the life of his child. To illustrate this, I heard some friends of ours (whom I will call Bill and Sheri) tell about a desperate call they received one evening from a mom. She begged them to come as quickly as they could. Our friends hurried to the home. When they arrived, the dad was in an uncontrolled frenzy. Bill and Sheri quickly learned that the son had a pregnant girlfriend. The mother feared that her husband's intense anger would lead to actions that would do more harm than good.

During the evening, a necessary lull in the heated conversation took place, and while they broke for a few minutes to allow the frazzled mom and dad to quickly tend to another matter, Sheri sat down at the family's personal computer. With permission to do so, she began to browse through it. Within moments a devastating discovery was made. Sheri, who happened to be a whiz with computers, punched a few buttons and the history tab revealed that someone had been accessing several Internet sites that featured pornography. Sheri brought the couple's attention to what she'd found, assuming that it was the son who had been dabbling in the raunchy material.

The mother quickly called her boy into the room and confronted him about the matter. With an expression of horror, he said nothing but looked at his dad with stark fear. The father stood quietly by, but the look on his face was that of total shock. Suddenly, the sickening truth fell on everyone in the room. The dad was the guilty party.

Everyone turned to look at him. He initially claimed innocence. When he realized there was no way out of the corner he was in, he began to weep. With a stream of tears running down his face, he admitted that in the deep of the night he'd been secretly surfing the web, indulging in the sin that had captured his mind. He had no idea that another pair of eyes was watching, and that he'd given an unintentional consent to his son to do the same and feed his youthful lust. The poison of pornography had not only corrupted the dad, but it also devastated his boy's life.

Bill and Sheri pointed to the father's indulgences as one of the routes by which Satan had gotten to their teenager. They prayed with the family and encouraged the dad to close the breach by repenting of his sin, ceasing his visits to the web traps, and making himself accountable to a counselor who would provide guidance in regard to lust.

This dad's story reinforces the steps we've covered in this chapter that we need to take in preparation for leading our children to Christ. To recap:

- First, yield our lives to Christ as Savior. As we follow Jesus, we can lead our children to Him.

- Next, daily pursue righteous living (holiness). Be on guard against the devil's infiltration of the heart and home. Take seriously the warning found in Isaiah 59:2: "Your iniquities have made a separation between you and your God, and your sins have hidden His face from you so that He does not hear." How can we ever see the critical needs of our kids if our spiritual eyes can't see over the wall of our own sin? And how can we be heard in heaven when our prayers are hitting the sound-deadening barrier of our iniquities?

With our hearts filled with God's presence through Christ and the confidence that comes from a clear conscience before Him, we can join "the Prayer Force" and do battle for the souls of our precious children.

4

What Is Effective Praying?

James 5:16 says, "The effective prayer of a righteous man can accomplish much." Next to the word "effective" in my New American Standard Bible (1995 edition), there's a reference to Genesis 18:22-33. That Old Testament passage reveals what "effective praying" is by sharing how Abraham questioned God multiple times in an effort to save the people of Sodom and Gomorrah. Abraham asked God if He would save the cities if 50 righteous people were found there. When God agrees, Abraham dropped the number to 45. God agrees again, and Abraham respectfully went for 30, then 20, and finally 10 righteous people. God agrees to not destroy Sodom and Gomorrah on account of even 10 righteous men. Unfortunately, God must not have found 10 righteous men because He got Lot and his family out and then destroyed Sodom and Gomorrah (Genesis 19).

The point of this well-known story of Abraham's repeated appeals is that effective praying has much to do with not giving up and being willing to go back to God with the same request over and over. To some of us, it may seem rude and feel awkward to approach God repeatedly about a matter, but we can take comfort in seeing that God wasn't offended by Abraham's recurring request. In fact, He seemed to willingly hear his humble and respectful servant each time Abraham asked.

We can also be encouraged to be persistent with our prayers by the parable Jesus shared about a widow who kept going to the king about a legal matter. Jesus told this story to inspire His followers to be boldly determined when it comes to praying:

In a certain city there was a judge who did not fear God and did not respect man. There was a widow in that city, and she kept coming to him, saying, "Give me legal protection from my opponent." For a while he was unwilling; but afterward he said to himself, "Even though I do not fear God nor respect man, yet because this widow bothers me, I will give her legal protection, otherwise by continually coming she will wear me out…" Hear what the unrighteous judge said; now, will not God bring about justice for His elect who cry to Him day and night, and will He delay long over them? I tell you that He will bring about justice for them quickly. However, when the Son of Man comes, will He find faith on the earth? (Luke 18:2-8).

The widow was commended for her unrelenting approach to the king about her legal situation. Her persistence became a picture of an attitude that gained Christ's admiration, which is revealed in His question, "When the Son of Man comes, will He find faith [like the widow's] on the earth?"

If a strong urgency about praying for your children has gripped your heart and mind, don't shrink back from taking your concern to the Lord and doing it often. And don't hesitate to keep asking Him for the same thing. The freedom He's given us to approach Him frequently is what encouraged me to say the same or similar prayers to Him every Wednesday as I prayed the lines in the lyric "Wednesday's Prayer" (see page 5). I often thought of Abraham's relentlessness and the widow's persistence as I prayed, and they gave me the courage to keep repeating my petitions until they were answered and then continue on with new ones.

What About Being a "Righteous Man"?

The words "righteous man" follows "effective prayers" in James 5:16, "the effective prayer of a righteous man can accomplish much," creates a short phrase that is very long on meaning. While maintaining effective prayers was something I was determined to do, I knew that being a "righteous man" was something only God could do in me. This realization made Abraham a doubly important biblical example.

Abraham had no righteousness of his own. Instead, God supplied Abraham with righteousness through his belief in Him, and Abraham accepted it (Genesis 15:6). Without God's provision of grace, Abraham would have had zero effectiveness in his prayers.

It was *Abraham's faith in God* that was the bank, so to speak, into which God deposited His righteousness. It's the same "bank account" that all of us have—in fact, the only one that will hold the righteousness God wants to give us. Even at this moment as you believe in Him, trust Him to credit you with the righteousness that you need to be a man who prays effectively. Your children need you to do it.

> Blessed are those whose lawless deeds have been forgiven, and whose sins have been covered. Blessed is the man whose sin the Lord will not take into account (Romans 4:7-8).

5

Why Fast?

Anyone who has fasted for a meal or for a month will testify to how much the flesh complains about the forsaking of food, even for the sake of adding effectiveness to prayer. Because fasting isn't easy or enjoyable, something of far greater importance than the taste for food must be the motivating factor to do it. If you're a parent, you don't have to look very far for that motivation.

As the concern for the salvation of your children grows in your heart and you face the increasing reality of how incredibly important it is for them to be healthy in spirit, soul, and body, you'll want to do more than casual or occasional sentence prayers for them. You'll want to cry out to God on their behalf. While doing so, you'll also want to show Him with more than your words how serious you are.

Are you seeing the desperate need to defy the flesh for the sake of this spiritual cause? For the first time ever, are you telling yourself at this moment that you're going to add fasting to your prayers? If so, I can tell you from experience that it's easier said than done but it's well worth the effort.

When I was sitting with my friend who had the wayward daughter and offering to join him in fasting every Wednesday for her, the words rolled off my tongue as easy as a bowling ball rolling down a hardwood lane. However, a few years had passed since I'd done any fasting, and by noon on the first Wednesday the hunger I felt reminded me of what a challenge I faced for the rest of the day and the upcoming Wednesdays. I do believe I could have consumed an entire cow down to the hooves...and then gnawed on the hooves.

My body was yelling so loudly in protest that I seriously considered calling my praying buddy to say, "Hey, you're on your own, man."

I readily admit that my affection for a good "gastronomical jubilee" is immense. If you've read any of my hunting books, especially *A Look at Life from a Deer Stand,* you know how much my mouth salivates just thinking of my wife's wonderful venison stew or delicious backstrap. Maybe you feel the same. If you're anything like me, one of your all-time favorite hymns is "When the Rolls Are Served Up Yonder, I'll Be There." Plenty of us would agree that the very thought of passing up any chance to feed is depressing enough to make us run out and grab a Big Mac and chocolate shake to appease our threatened taste buds.

Eating Is Not a Sin

We all know there's nothing wrong with eating food. In fact, our Creator designed us to need it, want it, and enjoy it. Genesis 1:29-30 clearly tells us what God has to say about eating: "Behold, I have given you every plant yielding seed that is on the surface of all the earth, and every tree which has fruit yielding seed; it shall be food for you; and to every beast of the earth and to every bird of the sky and to every thing that moves on the earth which has life, I have given every green plant for food." This passage mentions only plant life. However, after the flood in Noah's day, meat was added to mankind's menu:

> God blessed Noah and his sons and said to them, "Be fruitful and multiply, and fill the earth. The fear of you and the terror of you will be on every beast of the earth and on every bird of the sky; with everything that creeps on the ground, and all the fish of the sea, into your hand they are given. Every moving thing that is alive shall be food for you; I give all to you, as I gave the green plant" (Genesis 9:1-3).

Also in reference to food, 1 Timothy 4:4 says, "Everything created by God is good, and nothing is to be rejected if it is received with gratitude."

To put an exclamation point on His intention for people to enjoy food, God created us with a very well developed ability to taste. Most of us agree that our sense of taste adds an enormous amount of pleasure to life. Something tasty on my tongue, like Annie's "World-Famous Venison Chili," has been known to make me sing and dance around the kitchen!

While it's true that food is God's idea, and He has called it good for sustenance and pleasure, it has yet another great purpose. Food also helps fill our emotional need for companionship and fellowship. Since humankind has walked the earth, some of our deepest feelings of togetherness are experienced during the act of breaking bread together. One of Christ's most intimate moments with His disciples occurred at His last Passover meal (what we now refer to as the Last Supper) that He shared with them just prior to His crucifixion. In remembrance of that well-known meal and what it represents in terms of the sacrifice Christ would make for us, most congregations today serve "the Lord's Supper." The sacred rite of communion remains one of the most intense moments of sharing that Christians can experience. The piece of bread and the wine (often grape juice) binds our hearts together as we reflect on the crucifixion, the burial, and the glorious resurrection of our Savior.

If Food Is Such a Good Thing, Why Go Without?

So if food is such an important and enjoyable part of our existence, why then would God see our forsaking it as an honorable sacrifice? What purpose could it possibly serve? To appreciate this action that most folks dread to do, let's take a quick look at what fasting is and what it isn't.

6

What Is Fasting?

If you look up the word "fast" in Webster's Dictionary, you'll find that it has several meanings that are unrelated to the sacrifice of food:

- firmly fixed
- characterized by quick motion
- ahead of the correct time
- not easily disturbed (as in asleep)
- permanently dyed
- promiscuous

All these meanings of "fast" refer to the word's role as an adjective. However, the word is also a verb. In the verb form, Webster's shows only this meaning: "To abstain from food or to eat sparingly." While the word "intentionally" isn't included in the dictionary meaning of the verb form of "fast," most of us would agree that it would be appropriate to add it. It goes without saying that the action of fasting is something that is done *deliberately* and *by choice*.

While I don't personally know anyone who would inadvertently or accidentally fast, Annie claims she does. She would say that it's me. More than once I've overheard her telling her friends that I literally forget to eat when I get really busy with working. This makes her worry about what would happen to me if she weren't around. As frustrated as my dear wife can get about my tendency to overlook eating, she knows as well as I do that eventually I'll respond to the grumbling my stomach makes when I'm absentmindedly depriving it of food.

Fasting—Linked to Spirituality

There is one other thing about fasting that Webster's Dictionary doesn't include in its meaning, and it's surprising to me because it's the most obvious. Throughout history, especially biblical history, fasting has been connected to spirituality. In the Old Testament book of Leviticus, for example, the Israelites were given these instructions:

> This shall be a permanent statute for you: in the seventh month, on the tenth day of the month, you shall *humble your souls* and not do any work, whether the native, or the alien who sojourns among you; for it is on this day that atonement shall be made for you to cleanse you; you shall be clean from all your sins before the Lord (16:29).

The phrase "humble your souls" can also be translated "afflict your souls." The original meaning is referring to fasting *from* food. Psalm 35:13 removes any doubt that it is a reference to fasting from food. David wrote, "But as for me, when they were sick, my clothing was sackcloth; I humbled my soul with fasting, and my prayer kept returning to my bosom." (Also see Ezra 8:21-23.)

From these Scripture passages, it seems obvious that fasting was an activity that, in essence, was a kind of "soul chastening." While it was indeed an act of "body chastening," in that it taught the one who fasted a valuable lesson about physical endurance, the main benefit from fasting was in how it contributed to the person's communication and relationship with God.

There are nonspiritual reasons for people to fast. Just to mention two, they include the required 12-hour fast for cleansing purposes before a colonoscopy (bad memories!) and surgical procedures or not eating for a day or two before a class reunion to drop some midlife weight. While having a spiritual reason for fasting isn't required, most who fast regularly have a spiritual purpose in mind. The Bible contains plenty of examples of people fasting and the motivation for doing so.

When Grieving a Death

David and his men reacted to the deaths of Saul and Jonathan with fasting:

> David took hold of his clothes and tore them, and so also did all the men who were with him. They mourned and wept and fasted until evening for Saul and his son Jonathan and for the people of the LORD and the house of Israel, because they had fallen by the sword (2 Samuel 1:11).

An observation: In David's day, fasting was a customary way of showing that the spirit of the mourner was deeply pained. That custom would be doubly hard to follow these days because our tradition is quite the opposite. Today we "mourn and munch." Rarely will someone show up at a place where mourners gather without carrying a home-cooked dish to add to the table already brimming with food. To do so would be almost disrespectful.

When Feeling Deep Remorse

Paul the apostle is a good example of someone who responded to personal sin with fasting. After he was struck blind on the road to Damascus and made aware that he was committing a great sin against the Lord by persecuting His people, Paul was led into the city where he stayed "three days without sight, and neither ate nor drank" (Acts 9:9).

On a national level, corporate fasting because of sin also occurred:

Samuel spoke to all the house of Israel, saying, "If you return to the LORD with all your heart, remove the foreign gods and the Ashtaroth from among you and direct your hearts to the LORD and serve Him alone; and He will deliver you from the hand of the Philistines." So the sons of Israel removed the Baals and the Ashtaroth and served the LORD alone.

Then Samuel said, "Gather all Israel to Mizpah and I will pray to the LORD for you." They gathered to Mizpah, and drew water and poured it out before the LORD, and fasted on that day and said there, "We have sinned against the LORD" (1 Samuel 7:3-6).

When Sickness Comes to a Loved One

Second Samuel 12:16 records David's response to the terrible sickness that came to the son Bathsheba bore to him: "David therefore inquired of God for the child; and David fasted and went and lay all night on the ground." (Because I'm a dad who has stood in the hall of a hospital wondering if my child would come out of an emergency room alive, I'm grateful for the inspiration found in David's example of what parents can do for a gravely ill child.)

When the Leadership Needs Leading

The leaders in the church at Antioch sought God's directive regarding whom to send out as missionaries by praying and fasting:

> Now there were at Antioch, in the church that was there, prophets and teachers...While they were ministering to the Lord and fasting, the Holy Spirit said, "Set apart for Me Barnabas and Saul for the work to which I have called them" (Acts 13:1-2).

If the leadership of a congregation can fast and pray for direction for the entire body of believers, each believer can also fast and pray for the purpose of seeking God about a personal decision that must be made. I have my own example to offer on this one.

In 1974, I was a single, young singer/songwriter who was living in a house in Nashville with three other guys who shared the dream of being full-time musicians. The problem was that we didn't know if we were supposed to pursue music as a group or individually. And if we were to do it as a group, what would be our primary message? Was it to be evangelistic in content or were we to use music as a way to build up believers? We wanted more than anything to know what God wanted us to do. We knew that if He didn't guide us and anoint our efforts, whatever we endeavored wouldn't be rewarded with good fruit for our labor.

In July we all agreed to split up for two weeks and go somewhere to fast and pray for the purpose of knowing the Lord's will for us. I chose to go back to West Virginia to do my part. I knew of an abandoned house that sat in a field on a hilltop at a farm where I'd hunted while I was a teenager. I went there with my Bible, some containers of water, and a blanket. I planned to stay there until I heard from God.

To be candid, I didn't last long on that hilltop. I stayed nearly two days and endured the mosquitoes and rodents as much as I could. I decided to take my prayers and fasting back down the mountain to the comfort of my parents' home. Though I didn't follow through with my valiant plans to hibernate at the abandoned old house, I did feel in my heart that I could head back to Nashville with a clear answer from the Lord.

As it turned out, each of us struggled in similar ways to extend our fasting and praying to the two-week limit, yet each of us landed on the same runway when we came down from our lofty goal of a lengthy time of prayer and fasting. We met and heartily agreed that we were to be a group of musicians who would direct our ministry through music at building up believers. Our lyrics were to be saturated with Scripture-based admonitions and sound teaching...a directive I strive to follow to this day.

I should add that when I left the abandoned house and went back to my folks' to finish my two weeks of praying and fasting, I ran into someone who would become an important part of my future. She was a friend from high school who had traveled from Philadelphia to see her parents. Her name was Anne Williamson, and she would eventually become my bride. All the more reason for me to appreciate the trip to West Virginia to seek God!

Space doesn't allow the full telling of another personal example of fasting for the sake of knowing God's direction. Suffice it to say there used to be a barn on a farm south of Nashville where I spent a lot of time desperately asking God about what to do. It stood behind an old farmhouse (yes, another old farmhouse) where Annie and I first lived after we married in March of 1975. Sadly, that barn has long since been torn down and an office building stands on the ground it was on. I wish I had a piece of lumber that the barn was built with as a memorial to the place where I believe God spoke to my heart when I hungrily called on Him for guidance as a young husband and member of the freshly formed Christian music group Dogwood.

When Danger Looms

Fasting and praying for the sake of seeking God's protection is well illustrated in the eighth chapter of the book of Ezra. Carrying a large amount of gold and silver to the temple in the city of Jerusalem, the route that was taken by Ezra and the heads of the households, was very dangerous. Thieves and murderers were threats. In preparation for the risky journey, Ezra called for a fast. The outcome was very favorable for God's people, according to Ezra's report:

> I proclaimed a fast there at the river of Ahava, that we might humble ourselves before our God to seek from Him a safe journey for us, our little ones, and all our possessions. For I was ashamed to request from

the king troops and horsemen to protect us from the enemy on the way, because we had said to the king, "The hand of our God is favorably disposed to all those who seek Him, but His power and His anger are against all those who forsake Him." So we fasted and sought our God concerning this matter, and He listened to our entreaty (8:21-23).

Did you note the usage of the words "humble ourselves" in that passage? Once again, that term is used for fasting.

All these examples of reasons for adding fasting to praying reflect worthy causes for sure. Perhaps you've enlisted fasting for one of them. If so, you know how effective humbling yourself through intentionally foregoing food was in helping you focus on the need at hand and how God would meet it. Included in the various reasons to fast along with praying is the eternal spiritual welfare of our children—a cause that is more valuable than all the gold in the world.

7

What Fasting Is Not

In the context of this guide, it's important to maintain a biblical understanding and standard for fasting. To do so, it will be helpful to know what fasting is not.

1. *Fasting should not be for the purpose of dieting.* Fasting as part of a diet isn't wrong and can, with moderation, be helpful in losing or controlling weight. However, including weight loss in your reason for fasting as you pray for your children might compromise your focus on them. Nowhere in the Scriptures have I found a place where a secondary goal was added to a fast. Ezra didn't say, "I proclaimed a fast that we might humble ourselves before our God to seek a safe journey plus drop a few pounds."

2. *Fasting is not for those who keep God at a distance.* When it comes to gaining God's ear through fasting, if you are intentionally keeping God at a distance either by knowingly and habitually sinning or refusing to believe in Him, there is a sobering fact you should understand: God will not respond to the cries and fasting of those who prefer to wander through life without Him as their Lord:

> Thus says the LORD to this people, "Even so they have loved to wander; they have not kept their feet in check. Therefore the LORD does not accept them; now He will remember their iniquity and call their sins to account." So the LORD said to me, "Do not pray for the welfare

of this people. When they fast, I am not going to listen to their cry" (Jeremiah 14:10-12).

3. *Fasting is not a way to "twist God's arm."* Approaching God
with an attitude that you're going to make Him do something for
you by threatening Him with a "hunger strike" is an approach He
will not honor. Like a prison warden who doesn't allow hunger
strikes by inmates to force him into meeting their demands, God
will not be manipulated.

4. *Fasting is not honored when done with evil intent.* Suppose a
dad had a son whose character was being destroyed by the friends
he kept. In his fierce anger toward those who were leading his boy
astray, suppose the dad decided to fast and pray that God would
remove the bad guys from his son's life and, if necessary, remove
them through death. Do you think God would honor such a use
of fasting? No. And yet there are parents who have been so desperate to see a child freed from such deadly companions that they've
considered such drastic prayers. If this idea ever crosses your mind,
quickly read Acts 23:12-15. It's a very clear illustration of how
wrong and futile it would be:

> When it was day, the Jews formed a conspiracy and
> bound themselves under an oath, saying that they
> would neither eat nor drink until they had killed Paul.
> There were more than forty who formed this plot.
> They came to the chief priests and the elders and said,
> "We have bound ourselves under a solemn oath to taste
> nothing until we have killed Paul. Now therefore, you
> and the Council notify the commander to bring him
> down to you, as though you were going to determine
> his case by a more thorough investigation; and we for
> our part are ready to slay him before he comes near
> the place."

God can ultimately be credited for not allowing such a deviant plan to be successful. It seems safe to say that He put an exclamation point on His disapproval of the plot by protecting Paul with 200 soldiers, 70 horsemen, and 200 spearmen. The misuse of fasting with deadly intent wasn't honored in Paul's day, and it won't be honored today.

5. *Fasting is not to be a source of pride.* One of the first challenges I experienced after my friend and I added fasting to our prayers for our children was the feeling of guilt that came when I missed a Wednesday. Whether I would wake up and forget to do it or something came up, such as a business lunch I couldn't cancel, my heart would grind with guilt accompanied by self-loathing.

Thankfully, I finally realized that the guilt trip I was taking as a result of breaking "my law" was chaperoned by none other than the devil. As he led me down the path of guilt, he lived up to his title of accuser of the brethren (Revelation 12:10). He'd accuse me of several violations that were delivered to my mind through menacing whispers:

- "See there? You really don't love your children."

- "C'mon, Steve, don't kid yourself. You're a sad example of a dad who really cares about the eternal welfare of your kids."

- "You're a weakling."

- "You're just trying to impress God with your fasting."

- "Do you really think what you're trying to do will make a difference?"

- "Do you know how dumb you'll look if you don't go to lunch with your buddies or if you go and don't eat?"

- "Do you know how pompous you'll appear to your buddies if you skip lunch again this week?"

When the accusations stopped working (and some of them were quite effective until I caught on), the enemy tried flattery:

- "Look at you! You've gone a whole half-day without eating!"
- "You're awesome. You've done enough. God is surely amazed!"

Of all the whispers I heard from the enemy, without a doubt the one that had the most potential to do the greatest harm to the cause of effectively praying for my children came at the end of a fully completed day of fasting. With a voice that was very convincing I would often hear, "Well, now you can be proud of yourself." Why do these words hold such destructive power? Very simply, the devil knows very well that "God is opposed to the proud, but gives grace to the humble" (James 4:6). If I were to be prideful over having fasted for an entire day, I would set the Lord against me. That is not a situation healthy for me or my children.

When I was enticed by the devil's whispers to feel proud about fasting by skipping a meal or not eating for a full 24 hours, I knew I could find strength to resist that temptation by doing some loud whispering of my own. I would quote these words of John the Baptist: "[Jesus] must increase, but I must decrease" (John 3:30). For me to decrease required an act of my will. Like the sun rises when the earth bows in its rotation, when I consciously confessed that God alone is great and that I am good only because He lives in me, then the temptation to feel prideful about having done a day's fast would go away.

I would honestly be embarrassed to tell how many times I've repeated John's words to the enemy of my soul, who is also the enemy of my children. It seemed I had to relearn the lesson each week. It was a wearisome exercise, but thanks to God's provision of grace and strength, I was able to avoid falling to the bullet of pride.

6. *Fasting is not to be a religious law.* Very closely related to the error of being prideful about fasting is making it a religion, which can also be a goal-threatening mistake. It's not easy to admit, but it only took a few weeks of fasting on Wednesdays for me to begin to think that if I didn't faithfully follow through with the schedule, God would get mad and cut me off from His flow of grace. Basically, I made Wednesday prayer a law in my book, and I became quite religious about it.

My reaction to those times when I failed to "keep the law" was to mope around and feel bad (which was when the devil came at me with his wicked whispers that I mentioned earlier). I wasn't fun to be around when I was feeling defeated. Thankfully I managed to overcome the errant attitude. What made me realize that I was becoming obnoxiously religious about fasting was when I would silently look at other parents on Wednesdays who were eating while I was going without food. I would fleetingly think:

- Look at them stuffing their faces. They must not care about their children.

- They seem totally oblivious to the hell where their children might be heading.

- If they knew what I was sacrificing for the sake of my kids, they would feel bad and join me in this misery.

The religious spirit I entertained with my internal comments was the same one Jesus despised when He was among the "letter of the law" religious people here on earth. More than once He confronted those who were meticulous keepers of the law and put them in their place. For example, He had some strong words to say about those who were so religious that they tithed the tiny mint leaves but "neglected the weightier provisions of the law: justice and mercy and faithfulness" (Matthew 23:23). When it came to calling it what it was, Jesus held nothing back. In reference to the religious types, He used names that included "blind guides" and "hypocrites."

For me to be careful to keep my "Wednesday law" yet neglect to be kind with my thoughts about those around me was hypocritical. I fought this battle diligently, and still do after all these years. In order to help me be victorious over the temptation to be obnoxiously religious about fasting, I often turn to Matthew 6:16-18. This passage provides all the instruction I need to do fasting right:

> Whenever you fast, do not put on a gloomy face as the hypocrites do, for they neglect their appearance so that they will be noticed by men when they are fasting. Truly I say to you, they have their reward in full. But you, when you fast, anoint your head and wash your face so that your fasting will not be noticed by men, but by your Father who is in secret; and your Father who sees what is done in secret will reward you.

Another verse that helps when I'm tempted to be wrongly religious about fasting is Romans 6:14: "You are not under law but under grace." I came to the realization that a religious person—the kind Jesus didn't care for—would quickly get all bent out of shape if the law wasn't kept by him or anyone else. On the other hand, a person who chooses to live under grace instead of under the law won't act grumpy and irritable if for some reason the time of fasting was missed. Because I'd much rather accept God's grace than be spiritually and emotionally beaten by the "leather belt of the law," I refused to let it whip me when I missed a Wednesday fast.

Oh the feeling of freedom that came with realizing that because of grace, God wouldn't be mad at me if I couldn't or didn't "do Wednesday"! From that time on, I never took another guilt trip with the devil when I was unable to fast on my predetermined day. (I will admit the invitation to go with him was often extended.)

7. *Going without food is by no means a replacement for the finished work of Christ.* All that needs to be said about this truth is found in Ephesians 2:8-9: "By grace you have been saved through faith; and that not of yourselves, it is the gift of God; not as a result of works, so that no one may boast."

8

The Advantages of Fasting

There are at least two very beneficial advantages that fasting along with prayer can yield. One, it serves as a very effective reminder to pray. When we're awake and our day is underway, perhaps around nine o'clock in the morning, right in the middle of a moment when we're tending to one of the countless details that are necessary to accomplish our routine, our stomachs suddenly decide to protest the fact that we bypassed breakfast.

When that distinct, hunger-induced, attention-getting, sometimes audible gnawing in the belly is felt and/or heard, we can use it as a cue that it's time to stop and tug on the hem of God's garment, so to speak. Instantly our minds go to the reason for the hunger pangs, and then we can pause for at least a few moments to quietly pray for our children.

In time, as these challenging days of fasting and prayer are repeated, we learn that hunger pangs provide an advantage that is sort of like setting an alarm on a clock or on a smartphone that is programmed to sound with regularity throughout the day. You can go about your business without concern that you'll forget to pray because you can count on the frequent reminders the "Big Ben in your belly" will provide.

The second advantage that fasting with prayer yields is one that is of utmost importance even though, at first, it might sound overly mystical. Regular fasting helps open our spiritual eyes to the battles that rage against our children in the spirit world.

The basis for the acknowledgment that there is indeed a spiritual domain where supernatural war is waged is found in God's Word:

> Our struggle is not against flesh and blood, but against
> the rulers, against the powers, against the world forces
> of this darkness, against the spiritual forces of wicked-
> ness in the heavenly places (Ephesians 6:12).

Most of us don't argue with the premise that the supernatural is very real even though unseen. However, there are some who
don't accept the intensity of the impact that it can have on our tem-
poral existence. My parents *were not* among those who dismissed
the reality of the effect that the invisible had on the visible. They
fully embraced the truth that the "struggle is not against flesh and
blood," and they didn't hesitate to engage in the wrestling match
through prayer and fasting.

I came face-to-face with the kind of amazing insight a spiritually aware parent can have when I experienced a confrontation ini-
tiated by my mother. I'm convinced that it was through her intense
prayers and love-motivated fasting that she was able to see something she might have otherwise missed. Though the story that follows may sound a little farfetched, it is very true. It happened seven
years after Mom came into my bedroom and woke me up with her
"brave prayer" I mentioned in the first chapter. So here's my story.

I was twenty years old, a sailor in the Navy, and dabbling in
drugs. I came home unannounced one weekend on a three-day
leave from the Navy base in Norfolk, Virginia. When I got to the
house, my parents weren't there. It took only a couple of phone
calls to learn that they'd gone to a church convention in another
part of the state. Their absence left me alone in the house. Sitting
by myself in the kitchen, the idea came to me to treat myself to the
hashish that I'd carried home with me. I took out my pipe, put the
windows up to keep fresh air moving in and out, and proceeded to
smoke. Soon drug-induced paranoia was severe and ravaged my
mind with the fear that my folks would return unexpectedly and
catch me in my sin.

Though I knew what I was doing was wrong and I feared devastating my folks with the knowledge of my involvement in drugs, I continued my foolishness. Before putting my pipe away, I cleaned it using the fuzzy, white, flexible wires designed for the job. As I sat in a trancelike state in the kitchen, I eventually looked at the evidence of my wrong doing scattered on the table. I decided I needed to carefully hide the half-dozen, brown-stained cleaners. I methodically set out to conceal them using very deliberate, well-thought out steps.

- First I rolled and pressed the wire pipe cleaners into a tight, tiny ball and wrapped it in a paper napkin.
- Then I ripped the lid off of a Campbell's soup can that was in the garbage.
- I stuffed the napkin-covered pipe cleaners into the bottom of the can and put the lid on top. I added more napkins on top of the lid to the rim of the can.
- I opened the mouth of an empty, half-gallon milk carton and crammed the soup can containing the cleaners into the bottom. I stuffed some old newspaper on top of the soup can and fold-rolled the top of the wax milk carton like you would a paper sack.
- Taking all the trash out of the wastebasket under the sink, I put the "loaded" milk carton in the very bottom.
- I put the trash back on top of the milk carton and shoved the wastebasket back under the sink.

I felt quite confident that I'd covered all the steps necessary to conceal the evidence of my shenanigans. I returned to the Navy base. Two weeks later I went home again to see my family for the weekend. Sunday morning came, and once more it was time for me to head back to the ship. Before I got out of bed, my mother knocked and then came in. She sat down next to me on the edge of the bed and looked at me tenderly.

"Steve, are you going to go to church with us this morning before you leave for Norfolk?" she asked.

I wanted her to know my resistance to the idea, so I sighed, but I answered with a halfhearted, "Oh, I guess I will."

With a slight waver in her voice that always told me something serious and significant was about to be said, she spoke again. "Son, whose pipe cleaners were those in the trash can?"

I'm convinced that her question originated in heaven and reverberated in the caverns of hell. The enemy's camp was roused. Needless to say, I was in total shock. I had no time to prepare a defense. I was caught red-handed and had no other choice but to confess my sin.

Mom cried...I cried...all God's children in the Chapman household cried. I was almost relieved in a way. What Mom knew, Dad knew. There would be no more need to hide behind my false wall of fleshly, outward virtue I displayed when around my loved ones. Eventually, I came to see that it was God's mercy that allowed my mother's spiritual eyes to be opened to my transgression. It was His love and grace that had granted me the opportunity to let Him deal with my sin within the walls of earthly time instead of at the judgment that will follow my appointment with death (Hebrews 9:27).

I was also deeply grateful when my folks assured me that while they would never condone my actions, they loved me no matter what because I belonged to them. That day I learned what uncon-ditional love truly meant. Their kindness, which echoed God's kindness, led me to repentance. I changed direction...at least for a while (Romans 2:4).

Unfortunately, the wreck my life had become was a scene that I drove by and let fade in the distance. Sadly, it took one more nearly fatal spiritual incident on life's highway to get my full attention. I wandered once more into the camp of the enemy where there was plenty of partying to enjoy. I joined in, and once again my prayer-warrior parents went to God on behalf of their son who was drifting far from the shores of redemption. Armed with a regimen of daily praying and frequent fasting, my parents "stormed the gates of hell" in an effort to persuade Almighty God to intervene and reclaim the soul of their only begotten son.

Amazingly enough, the person God used to rattle the cage of my stubborn heart was someone whom none of the Chapman family would have ever expected, especially my parents.

9

The Vestal Intervention

As promised in chapter 2, here's the story of one of the major ways God answered my parents' prayers and honored their sacrifice of nourishment on my behalf. I offer this candid account to encourage you to keep praying for your children. God has a way of surprising us with how He works on our behalf.

Answered Prayer

In the 1960s, one of our family's favorite Christian music groups was the Happy Goodman Family. Their Southern Gospel-style more than satisfied our taste for the hand-clapping, foot-tapping, heart-changing songs we so enjoyed. When we performed as The Chapman Family group, we'd often incorporate their songs into our repertoire.

As far as we were concerned, the Happy Goodman Family had hung the musical moon. We were avid fans and never missed seeing them when they came to our part of the country. They were celebrities, and I assumed they would always remain a group of folks we would know only at a distance. But prayer changes things—especially my mother's prayers.

In the fall of 1972, when I was discharged from the Navy, I had a well-used Chevrolet Biscayne. I left Virginia Beach in it with discharge papers in hand, about $150 in my wallet, my 1950, J-50 Gibson guitar in its case in the backseat, as well as a heart full of wanderlust that led me anywhere the wind blew.

I basically lived in my car and totally enjoyed the return to a life free from the disciplines and accountability that the military represented. Even though I'd been previously confronted by God through my mother about my preference for the fun illegal drug use offered, I left the base looking to buy the first nickel bag of "weed" I could find. I was like a dog returning to its vomit.

It wasn't too many miles down the road that I found what I was looking for. During the next few months, I once again dabbled in dope. But deep inside me was a nagging feeling that what I was doing was not only dumb, but, more importantly, it wasn't pleasing to God. I had to push aside a lot of good sense just to enjoy the pleasures of sin that had captured my heart and my life. As hard as I tried, I never felt totally at ease while engaging in sin in such an abandoned way.

As I wandered around the states in my Biscayne, nearly broke and stopping at Interstate rest areas to find picnickers willing to trade a sandwich for a song, I drove through the state of Kentucky. As my tires rolled across the beautiful roads of the Blue Grass State, I entered the town of Madisonville. When I saw the sign, it suddenly hit me that it was the hometown of the Happy Goodman Family.

Not having a GPS or a smartphone for an address search, I stopped at a phone booth and looked up the address for the offices of the Goodmans. It wasn't a huge town, so they were easy to find. When I pulled up to the building, I saw their familiar tour bus sitting nearby. I felt very excited to be on the grounds of the group I'd so admired while growing up in my West Virginia home.

I sat in the parking lot and debated whether or not to go inside. I needed a good reason to enter their world. I didn't have to search my mind too long to find a pretty good one. If you remember, earlier I noted that I assumed I would never get to meet the celebrated Happy Goodman Family. That assumption was thrown out when, at a mere 17 years old, I got to be their warm-up act at a concert they did at the Red Jacket, West Virginia high school gymnasium.

That night I sang two gospel songs I'd written. One of them was titled "I'm Not Worried About the Natural Man." After I sang it, one of the Goodman brothers, Sam, stepped to the microphone and told the crowd of about 700 people that the Goodmans would seriously look at recording the song on one of their future albums. It was an absolutely unforgettable experience to hear his words! I left the building feeling sure that, as they say, "the rest would be history." I had great hopes I would find a place in the Southern Gospel Music world. But that's not what happened.

Time went on, and so did life. I graduated from high school, had a year of college, joined the Navy, and was discharged. By the time I found myself sitting in the parking lot of the Goodmans' offices, I was a much different person than the group would remember. I'd embraced a lifestyle that resulted in becoming a long-haired, ragged, bellbottom-wearing, dope-smoking, rock-and-roll loving, antiestablishment, unkempt, smelly hippie.

I was definitely practicing what I'd preached in my song the Goodmans heard me sing back in Red Jacket, I wasn't concerned in the least about my "natural man." By that I mean I was doing one of the things die-hard hippies were known for back in the early 1970s—avoiding personal hygiene, which included socially important things like showers, deodorant, shaving, and general personal grooming.

Knowing that I basically looked and smelled bad enough to resemble some form of the wrath of God, and knowing it probably would be better to drive away unnoticed, something compelled me to go inside. I figured my best reason for doing so was to ask about the song that had been passed over. So I looked in my rearview mirror and ran my fingers through my curly, shoulder-length, freak flag (a name for long hippie hair at the time) in an attempt to make it look as presentable as possible. I did the nose under the arm test, but I really couldn't tell if I smelled rank, due to my olfactory system having likely been ruined by the stench of smoke of various types.

With my heart pounding, I walked through the glass door at the front of the Goodman Sound Studio. The building was well lit, and there were several office doors on both sides of the long hall I walked down. As I passed each one, the occupants looked up, startled, as if a burglar had surprised them. I'm sure they weren't used to seeing someone in their workplace who appeared to have wandered away from the muddy fields of Woodstock.

After passing several doors, I looked into the last one on the right. Standing there in casual, off-stage clothes was Rusty Goodman. I nearly fainted from starstruck syndrome. He looked up at me, and I was surprised by how unshaken he seemed by my very out-of-the-ordinary presence.

"May I help you?" he asked, his strong voice projecting with resonance.

"Yes, sir," I answered with the respect due such a legend in the Gospel Music field.

At that instant, Rusty's brother, Sam, came to the door and stood by me. He too was completely cordial and inquisitive about their unexpected visitor.

"What's your name, buddy?"

Sam's voice warmed my heart. I'd heard it so often on stage as he sang, spoke between songs, and delivered some of the best well-timed humor of anyone I knew who held the position of performer.

"I'm Steve Chapman." I could see the name rang a bell in their minds. I could also see the bit of bewilderment on their faces when they realized who I was. I didn't wait for either of them to ask why I was in the building or to comment on what I looked like. I went ahead and told them what I wanted to say.

"A few years ago I warmed up your group in Red Jacket, West Virginia. I sang a song that night that y'all seemed interested in." I gave them the title of my song.

Both of them seemed to instantly remember me and their reaction at the concert.

"Man, you've changed!" Sam said, bypassing the subject of the song and what had happened to the idea of possibly recording it. Instead, he inquired about the obvious transformation I'd made in my appearance. I related where I'd been since the Red Jacket event, and within a minute or two they were caught up on my journey. They could easily see that I had chosen a path that took me down a friendship with "the world," but they didn't challenge my looks or my state of mind. They remained friendly.

Before we got back to the topic of my song, the hall suddenly filled with people who seemed to be frantic about something. I quickly learned by their exchanges that photographers were coming the next day to take pictures of the building I was standing in. It was brand-new and contained their newly constructed, full-service recording facility.

Amid the commotion, I bid farewell to Sam and Rusty and thanked them for seeing me. I turned to walk out to my car when I heard Sam say to Rusty, "We gotta get someone to clean up around the outside and clear the construction debris so the photographer won't get it in the shots." What I heard wasn't just a statement about their need for a cleanup crew. I heard a chance to maybe make a few dollars to help me get down the road. Without rehearsing a pitch for my services, I wheeled around and said, "Mr. Sam! I'm your man for the clean-up job. I'll do it for whatever you want to pay me. I could use some cash."

Sam's smile was always huge and fun to see. He flashed his big friendly grin as he walked toward me with his hand out to shake mine.

"You're hired, young man. Just make it look spiffy out there, and get it done before the end of the day, if possible. I'll make sure you get some green money for your labor."

I rolled up the sleeves of my flannel shirt and immediately got busy. I did the work of three men as fast as I could. I carried away remnants of 2 x 4s, drywall end pieces, and roofing shingles. I picked up a bucket's worth of unused nails, cleared pop cans and candy wrappers, and went the extra mile by cleaning the dust off the windows and spraying the mud off the brick. By the time I got through around seven o'clock that evening, the building looked picture ready.

Sam came back and was very complimentary about my work. As he handed me several twenty-dollar bills, he surprised me with a question that I'm sure was prompted by pity.

"Do you have a place to stay tonight?"

I didn't except for my Chevy Biscayne Hilton. "No, sir."

"We've got a room with a bed in it and a bathroom on the back-side of our old office building if you'd like to use it."

Without thinking more than a second about the idea of sleeping in a bed that didn't have door handles and window cranks on each end, as well as a bathroom that didn't require a key from a gas station attendant, I said, "I'd be grateful for the room."

When the next morning came and I reappeared at the office building, those who had caught a glimpse of me the day before were even more surprised to see me still around. Sam arrived and greeted me with his big, infectious smile. Then he completely surprised me with another offer.

"Steve, you did such a great job sprucing up the outside of this building. Would you like to stay on for a little while? We could use the help around here right now."

How I wished that my mother, dad, and sister could have been standing there when *the* Sam Goodman offered me a job! When I called later to tell them about it, the joy in their voices was a delight to hear. They could hardly believe it.

Though the job was temporary, I might as well have been offered the position of president of the United States! I felt so humbled, and I was definitely grateful for the labor. There was only one hitch in the deal that Sam didn't know about. Behind the mask of my respectful demeanor and willingness to work hard was a residual hunger for the pleasures of sin, especially the substance type. I didn't reveal it as I took Mr. Sam up on his offer.

I settled into the backroom at the old office and conscientiously did my job as groundskeeper, janitor, and whatever else needed done, such as loading their massive sound system and boxes of long-play record albums in the bays of the big, shiny bus each Thursday as they readied to hit the road. I couldn't have been in a better spiritual environment than being around a group of gospel music singers whose kindness was even greater than their fame. However, as good as their influence was on me, it didn't squelch the want I had for an occasional buzz from some illegal smoke.

While the Goodmans were away on their short tours, I managed to connect with a few locals who would supply bags of stuff to roll for smoking. I was as discreet as I could be, yet all the while remembering the pipe-cleaner incident with my mother.

I wasn't aware that all along, as I traveled about in my lostness, my parents were praying fervently with hunger pangs that God would send someone to me who would speak the truth, who would love me back to some good sense, and who would be a strong enough influence that I would finally listen. They longed for me to have the kind of spiritual experience that would result in breaking through the darkness I was in and finding the light of God's everlasting love. As I've mentioned, what they never dreamed would happen was who God would use as a messenger of His redemption.

While God had used Sam and Rusty's graciousness to draw me in to stay at Madisonville, it was Vestal Goodman, the wife of the elder brother, Howard, whom God most effectively used to confront and challenge my wayward heart. I'll never forget when and where it happened.

We were standing in the same hallway I'd first walked down at their offices about three months earlier. As if God Himself stood before me, Vestal spoke with boldness and great love as she shook me back to the reality that He wasn't going to abandon His intention to save me from the grip the world had on me. With a finger lovingly tapping me on my chest, she looked into my bloodshot eyes and delivered words straight from heaven. They were few, but they were powerful: "Steve, I know what you're doing, and God knows too. You need to stop it right now, turn around in your heart, and go home to Jesus."

And that's all it took—well, that and all the prayers raised on my behalf. Vestal Goodman, the woman who was loved across the nation by countless fans of the Goodmans' music and who was known for her amazing voice, had shown true love to a long-haired, wandering hippie. She spoke truth to me as though I were her own. I was speechless as she pinched my bearded cheek, smiled, and then headed down the hall.

It's been more than 40 years since that momentary-yet-eternally important intervention in the hallway with sweet Vestal. And since that pinch on my cheek, I've not imbibed in drugs or drink or any other enticements that were so attractive to me at that time. Not only did I stop using immediately, but I promptly flushed my stash down the toilet. And to the Goodmans' great satisfaction and public-relations relief, I went straightway to get a haircut and buy some new clothes.

Needless to say, I will be forever grateful for how God led me to Madisonville, Kentucky, and to such loving people as the Happy Goodman Family. The four original members of the quartet are all deceased now, but I like to imagine the music they're making in heaven. I don't have a death wish, but I do look forward to hearing them again. I not only want to enjoy their singing, I want to thank each one of them for showing me such mercy and grace. And I want to make sure they understand that they were the totally unexpected answer to my parents' prayers about their prodigal son.

The following lyric paints a picture of what took place in my life so long ago.

Send Somebody

Another teardrop hits the table
Breaks the silence in the room
And a cry goes up to heaven from a broken heart
She's been prayin' all these years for
A rebel son who's lost his way
She doesn't know how to reach him,
　　she doesn't know where to start

She prays, "Will You send somebody?
He can't make it on his own
Lord just send somebody
To tell him You're his only hope
I don't have to know their name,
　　and I don't have to see their face
All that matters is that he hears about
　　Your saving grace
Lord, will You send somebody?"

It's a cold night in the city
He turns his collar to the wind
And his pockets are as empty as his lonely soul
He goes up to a stranger and says,
"Do you have some change to spare?"
While a thousand miles away his mother
　　whispers soft and low...

"Will You send somebody?
He can't make it on his own
Lord, just send somebody
To tell him You're his only hope
I don't have to know their name,
      and I don't have to see their face
All that matters is that he hears about
      Your saving grace
Lord, will You send somebody?"

And then a stranger on the street says,
      "I have more than change to give
Let me tell you about the One who died so that
      you can really live!"

As his mama prays...
"Will You send somebody?
He can't make it on his own
Lord, just send somebody
To tell him You're his only hope
I don't have to know their name and
      I don't have to see their face
All that matters is that he hears about
      Your saving grace
Lord, will You send somebody?"[6]

10

Guidelines for Fasting

If you're ready to add fasting to your prayers, allow me to share my recommendations for how and when to do it. In no way do I wish to imply that these guidelines are the best and the only ones to follow. They have worked well for me, and hopefully they'll give you some helpful ideas about *what* to fast, *how* to fast, and *when* to fast.

What to Fast…the Main Consideration

While there are biblical precedents, such as Jesus' 40-day fast and "Daniel's fast," the sacrifice you make for your kids should be done according to your own convictions and a wise assessment of your circumstances (Matthew 4; Daniel 1:8-13). The main consideration when deciding whether to fast from food is to answer the question, "Are you medically able to fast?" If you have a known health problem that would preclude you from significantly changing your dietary habits, you should first consult your physician before fasting. If, for example, you struggle with diabetes and regular food intake is essential to your health regimen, fasting food would be dangerous and not advised. Instead, you can forego something other than food, and the choices are numerous.

Alternative Things to Fast

The list of nonfood items people can sacrifice as they pray is probably as long as the list of people who would do it. It's not unreasonable to say that everyone has a strong appetite for something they enjoy other than food. For some it may be an activity they like to do that feeds a longing in their lives, for others it might be something they love to hear or see that nourishes their soul. To attempt to name what all these possibilities are would require more space than I have, so I'll give just a few examples.

One of the most creative replacements for fasting food was something I heard about from a gentleman I met in an East Coast state. After one of our concerts, he informed me that he was medically unable to fast meals, but he had decided to fast an entire season of deer hunting to let God know he was serious about his prayers for his children.

Being an avid deer hunter myself, I was greatly impressed with what he'd chosen to fast. I met him while he was nearing the end of his state's deer season, so I personally commended him for such a courageous decision and follow-through. I also admitted that he sure did know how to mess with a fellow deer hunter's ego because I felt like a spiritual wimp when he told me what he was willing to give up. Of course, I was attempting a little bit of humor with him, but whenever I recall our conversation I still feel challenged regarding what level of sacrifice I'm willing to make for the sake of my prayers. Also, I've wondered what long-term effect such a major sacrifice had on his children's lives. I'm quite sure it was very positive. Annie agrees and quips, "By now his kids are probably missionaries...on Mars!"

Another nonfood item that was fasted by a gentleman in a Southern state was also creative, but it presented an especially hard challenge. Annie and I were in concert at an auditorium in Georgia. During the first half of the evening, we sang our song "Wednesday's Prayer" (see the front of this book). As part of the verbal setup for the song, we told the audience about the influence that praying with fasting can have on the lives of children. We also told them that sacrificing something is an effective way to let God know how serious they were about praying, and we suggested fasting food. We finished the concert and then closed the evening. Following the dismissal, a fellow came to us and told us something we've never forgotten.

"When you talked about praying and fasting for your kids," he began in his Southern drawl, "I realized I really needed to do it. My kids have gone wild, and I'm at a total loss about what to do. So I just wanted you to know I'm gonna try this fasting thing and kick my prayers into the next gear." He removed a pack of cigarettes from his coat pocket and continued. "And you know what? I started during the break this evening with giving up something to let God know I'm serious about this. I've been a smoker for several years. I went outside at break to light up, and as I took out my lighter I heard these words in my mind, 'Every time you get the urge to smoke, instead you could pray for your kids!'" The man smiled. "It wasn't easy to put my cigarettes back in my pocket, but I did. And as much as I like to smoke, which is over a pack a day, you can bet my kids are gonna get prayed for a whole lot."

Annie and I shook the man's hand and offered a blessing to him that God would help him be faithful to his gutsy decision. We also thanked him on behalf of his children for showing such a display of love. Because we know some folks who are heavily addicted to the nicotine in cigarettes, in chewing tobacco, and in "dip," we're very aware that it can be a stronghold for a person. That dad inspired us.

There are things that can be fasted that can be just as tough for others. For example, some of us would cringe in pain at the idea of giving up political talk radio or a cable news channel. Many Americans feed on the flow of information on these shows the way ravenous teenagers consume pizza. Just the thought of going without the nonstop banter between show hosts, guests, and callers even for half a day makes the right side of our bodies go into a spasm (or left side, depending on your political leanings).

Then there's technology that can be sacrificed. What if, let's say, you put your smartphone on the shelf for 24 hours—or even just 12 hours—and, as a fast, avoided it completely. Could you do it? Would you even dare? If you do try it, I'm sure the reminders you'd get to pray for your children would be frequent and pronounced. Every time you habitually dig into your pocket for the device or your fingers twitch like they need to type out a text, you could use it as a cue to whisper a prayer for those you love.

For some of us, fasting a favorite TV series or daily show that we "live to see" could be a good choice. It's hard to imagine how tough it would be for some of us fellows to get home from church on a Sunday in October and instead of plopping down in an easy chair in the den with a plate full of lunch and flipping on a football game, we'd go to our man cave and pray for our family...at least through the first half. The withdrawals we would feel might sting at the time, but oh what a gift to our loved ones.

For others, not watching golf, baseball, basketball, or any other source of on-air competition would definitely compete with our longing for the "media meal" that is fed each Sunday to fans like you and me.

The nonfood item that you might consider sacrificing may not be among these mentioned. What would it be for you? Likely, it will take only a second or two for you to think it through and come up with an answer. The one thing you enjoy the most that's not found in a pantry or in a refrigerator would be the top candidate. The question is, are your children and their spiritual welfare worth the sacrifice?

When to Fast…Choosing a Time Frame

Once you've made the personal choice of *what* to fast, choosing *when* to do it is the next thing to decide. This too is a decision based on what best fits you and your life. Here are some options to consider that can be adapted to whatever you decide to fast.

A Full-Day Fast

As I mentioned in the introduction to this book, my friend and I chose Wednesdays as our day to fast and pray. We picked a mid-week day for two reasons, and both are worth considering as you choose a day for adding a fast to your prayers.

Minimal energy output: Because of our relaxed work schedules, neither of us had to expend a lot of physical energy. While hunger wasn't easy to tackle any way we went about it, it seemed more doable when we were able to conserve our strength throughout the day.

Minimal mental distractions: Because our minds weren't completely consumed by the demands that our work responsibilities put on us during Wednesdays, we could give more attention to what the day was all about. While Wednesday worked very well for us, we were aware that the day that was chosen wasn't really the main point. Instead, what really mattered was what the day meant to us as dads who were concerned about our kids.

The Time Frame

The time frame we set for our fast was from after dinner on Tuesday evening until dinnertime on Wednesday evening. On average, our fast lasted 22 to 24 hours, depending on when dinner ended on Tuesday and when it was served on Wednesday. Our goal was always to go a full 24 hours, but we intentionally made that a flexible rule. We knew well that we had to allow some give-and-take in our plan due to everyone's schedules and the challenges when the entire family wanted to sit down for a mealtime.

When people ask me, I often recommend Wednesday as the day of choice, admittedly for a selfish reason. There's something deeply inspiring about knowing that I would be joining with a host of others on the same day in praying sacrificially for our children. The camaraderie I feel with other parents would be encouraging to say the least. However, I'm well aware that Wednesdays won't work for everyone.

A friend of ours chose to do a full-day fast each week on Monday. He says that for some reason it feels right to follow a busy Friday to Sunday weekend with refocusing on his prayers for his children. Another dad decided that Thursday was his best day to add a fast to his prayers because of his odd work schedule. Only you know what day would work best for you. You might even try different days to determine which is best for you.

Half-Day Fast

For some, a half-day fast is a good time frame because of the type of lifestyle they lead. For example, I have a friend whose work includes lunch meetings nearly every day both at his office and at local eateries. It's much too awkward for him to not order food and have to answer questions about why he's not partaking when the meeting starts. For him, starting his fast when he wakes up in the morning (or after dinner the night before) and going until lunch time is his best option.

For some, a half-day of fasting fits well into their schedules because of the amount of energy they have to expend while doing their work or, in the case of young parents, chasing after rambunctious children for hours on end.

If a half-day fast works for you for these reasons or any other, or if it simply appeals to you because the time frame sounds more doable, then go for it. Just remember, don't feel guilty if your choice is a half-day fast. The devil would like nothing more than to make you feel less accomplished than others as you pray for your children. Don't let him belittle your choice of when or how long to fast. Refuse to wallow in the mire of the enemy's ridicule and proceed with confidence that you're doing your best when it comes to bringing your children before the Lord in prayer.

Single Meal Fast

My buddy and I found out very quickly what a formidable challenge starting with a full day of fasting could be, but the desperation to see his daughter's life turn around was great enough that it didn't matter. Looking back, if we would have thought about how tough it would be to go from eating every day—sometimes four times a day—to not eating at all for 24 hours, we might have opted to start with a shorter fast or start with a shorter fast and work up to a longer one. With this in mind, if you've never done a full-day fast, a single meal fast is a good place to start.

To determine which meal to forego, consideration should be given to which meal represents the greatest challenge. For example, there are some whose absolutely favorite meal of the day is breakfast, and to think about bypassing it gives them the jitters. This would be all the more reason to consider breakfast as the meal to fast simply because it adds an extra measure of seriousness to the purpose.

For others, fasting lunch works well because their lifestyle allows it. Perhaps the day is spent working alone or maybe traveling, and for those reasons having breakfast and not eating again until dinnertime in the evening works well. If you're wondering if this is sufficient in letting God know you're serious about your praying, try it once and you'll find there'll be plenty of belly grumbling between breakfast and dinner to remind you to pray.

Other Helpful Tips for Fasting

Avoid Pre-Fast Gorging

When I first began the journey of fasting with praying for 24 hours, it didn't take but a few Wednesdays to realize how tempting it was to stuff myself before I retired on Tuesday night to avoid feeling so hungry the next day. I knew to do so, however, would defeat my purpose. What I needed on Wednesdays were the attention-getting hunger pangs in the belly to remind me of the need my kids have for prayer. If my stomach was still full from the previous evening's four-course picnic I consumed just before bedtime, I was less likely to get the reminders until later in the day.

Pre-fast gorging for the purpose of avoiding the mid-fast belly groans is tempting to do, even for those who choose a single-meal fast. For example, piling on some extra pancakes at breakfast and grabbing a few more strips of bacon in order to not feel so ravenous during a lunch-only fast seems like a good idea. But remember, doing so eliminates one of the best advantages of fasting—the memory-jogging belly groans that can be felt (and sometimes heard) during the course of the day that says, "It's time to pray for your kids!"

When You Completely Forget

I also discovered in my first few weeks of fasting that it was not that hard to forget my commitment to Wednesday's prayer and fasting. Several times I bounced out of bed not realizing what day it was, grabbed a granola bar and coffee, and headed off down the road in my pickup...and then suddenly remember what I'd done. By then I was a few miles and burps down the highway. When this happened, I grappled with the guilty feelings that always came until I called on God's grace to help me refuse the scolding from the devil. I then set my sights on fasting the next day instead.

Flexibility Is a Must

In this quest for maintaining a scheduled time of serious, sacrificial prayer, flexibility is a must. As mentioned earlier, I learned right away that anything can happen to tamper with my plans. Sometimes a business lunch fell on Wednesday, or relatives arrived unexpectedly at noon, or friends from a faraway city called as they were passing through town and wanted to meet up for lunch. When circumstances such as these that were beyond my control and completely changed things, it was time to make alternate plans. If I knew in advance that Wednesday would be blocked, I opted for fasting on Tuesday. Sometimes I had to spread the process over a two-day period (fasting until noon both days).

However it's done, denying the flesh for a season to attain a spiritual goal sometimes requires a willingness to accommodate the rest of the world around us. Oddly enough, when a parent sees some positive results in their children that praying with fasting brings about, they may develop a firm resistance to revising their schedule. Still, adaptability will be a valuable virtue. (Of course, if fasting becomes impossible during a particular week, by all means don't forget to pray and then look ahead to the next week.)

Taking It on the Road

Annie and I travel extensively as concert artists and speakers, and when our children were still at home they went with us most of the time. Though we were rarely on the road midweek, there were some tours that spanned upwards of eight to ten days. That meant that my Wednesday fast would have to be done while traveling.

I found that most of the time my planned fast could still be done while away from home, and sometimes with less distractions. This was true because we were responsible for mealtimes, and the only two people who knew Annie and I were fasting were our children. There were times when event sponsors would want to offer breakfast or lunch on a Wednesday, and we wouldn't refuse their gracious hospitality. We simply knew in our hearts that it was time to adjust. You may find that fasting while traveling might be just as doable, if not more, for the same reasons. There's no need to completely abandon your prayer plan when the wheels are rolling.

One side benefit of having to alter our fasting plans from time to time while traveling is worth mentioning to those of you who hit the road with your family. Whether your trip is for business or pleasure, you'll discover that your children, like ours, will get a firsthand lesson on what it means to exercise flexibility. Our two kids learned by observation that "the law" didn't apply to our decision to fast and that grace was vital to maintaining a right attitude about the regimen. The interesting thing was that by the time they were in their mid-teens, they came to count on our sacrificial prayers for them. A few times we could tell they were a little concerned when we missed a Wednesday.

Be a Courteous Faster

If you're fasting alone as a parent, be sure to let your spouse know your plan in terms of the time frame. If your wife needs to plan a mealtime that accommodates your fast, it would be gracious to let her know. If you extend your fast for some reason, also let her know as much in advance as possible. The goal is to avoid inconveniencing your spouse with the burden of your prayer and fasting choice.

Wash Your Face

Speaking from experience, as I've already mentioned, it's easy to be prideful about fasting. It's tempting to want others to know about our sacrifice on behalf of our children. However, if we allow that, we'll weaken the weapon that sacrificial praying can be against the enemies that war against our kids. What is the solution? Thankfully, it's in the Scriptures. Instead of heralding the fact that we're fasting, we're to be careful to follow these instructions given by Jesus:

> Whenever you fast, do not put on a gloomy face as the hypocrites do, for they neglect their appearance so that they will be noticed by men when they are fasting.

Truly I say to you, they have their reward in full. But you, when you fast, anoint your head and wash your face so that your fasting will not be noticed by men, but by your Father who is in secret; and your Father who sees what is done in secret will reward you (Matthew 6:16-18).

If a period of fasting is done well, no one except your immediate family will know about it. Being repaid by the heavenly Father for what is done secretly should be, by all means, plenty of reward. If there is a prize to be given from God for your sacrifice, may it be that His light will shine in the lives of your children.

11

When to Pray

If you choose a specific day of the week to fast and focus your prayers on your children, you might ask the same questions I did when I began doing it.

- "During my prayer day, when can I pray?"
- "Is it okay to have a routine for prayer?"
- "Do I need to stop what I'm doing, go to my knees in the classic position of prayer, and bow my head?"

While these were legitimate questions to ask, I came to realize they had roots in the fear of doing prayer wrong. I certainly didn't want to weaken my efforts by failing in the areas of posture and timing when I prayed. Thankfully, some important biblical passages were helpful in calming my fear.

"During my chosen prayer day, when can I pray?" Two encouraging and comforting scriptures serve to answer very clearly the question of when we can pray:

- The eyes of the LORD are toward the righteous and His ears are open to their cry (Psalm 34:15).

Note that this verse contains no qualification regarding when God's eyes are watching or when His ears are listening. Thankfully, there's no shingle hanging on God's door that says: "Listening Hours 9 to 5/Closed on Holidays." Instead, His listening ear is open 24/7. For that reason, whenever you'd like to or need to pray, it is acceptable to God.

- Behold, He who keeps Israel will neither slumber nor sleep (Psalm 121:4).

Because God is Spirit and not affected by fatigue the way we humans are, He's *always* awake. What an incredible comfort to know that no matter what time of day it is, if I sense an urgency to pray about someone or a situation I encounter I don't have to awkwardly say, "Uh, excuse me God. I hate to wake You up, but can I talk to You about something?" To know He is *always* aware of my need is a blessing beyond measure, especially when it comes to feeling the weight of responsibilities that come with being a dad.

"Is it ok to have a routine for prayer?" Though it is biblically true that we have access to God's ear at all times, most of us don't live our lives open-ended in terms of our daily schedules. We are beings who make schedules, write "to do" lists, mark calendars, and, in this high-tech age, enter digital reminders in our smartphones and gadgets that beep or bark like a dog (at least mine does) to jog our memories about things we're responsible to do. Simply put, we seem to willingly embrace our relationship with time, and we accept the fact that the hands of the clock significantly influence how we live.

Speaking of clocks, most of us have an alarm that we set each night and respond to when it yells out the morning wake-up call. Also, a very large percentage of us have watches on our arms or at least carry a communication device somewhere on our person that shows the time. Therefore, as it pertains to what we do in a 24-hour period of our existence, we humans seem content to operate within the structured and predictable ticks of the clock.

If you are one who likes to pray at a predictable time and place, you're normal. And you'll be glad to know that you're in good company because even Jesus appreciated having a regular prayer routine. That fact is revealed in Luke 22:39: "He came out and proceeded *as was His custom* to the Mount of Olives." Whether or not Jesus went there at a specific time each day, week, month, or year is not fully known, but it seems that at least He went often enough to understand the value of having some level of regularity when it came to His schedule. For this reason, I say to any parent who wants to set aside any specific day, hour, or even minute of the week to pray and fast for your children, the freedom to do so is biblically granted.

"Do I need to stop what I'm doing, go to my knees in the classic position of prayer, and bow my head?" While I definitely believe that reverently kneeling and audibly verbalizing prayer is a wonderful thing and should be done as often as possible, I candidly admit that this was rarely a prayer posture I took. Though Wednesday was usually my "weekend" and I hoped to have less to do, very often within a few minutes after waking up one of the many cares of life would grab my attention. The next thing I knew I was off and running with my mind on anything but praying. Hunger pangs would remind me to pray. When this happened, I had to resist the temptation to feel guilty that I wasn't on my knees in prayer. Thankfully, there was an alternative that worked for me, and I'm sure it will work for anyone whose prayer day quickly fills up with stuff to do. Instead of being a "kneeler," I became a "weaver." That is, I learned to weave my prayers into the open moments of my day that I found between being a husband, a dad, the manager of a company, songwriter, performer, author, public speaker, hunter, and frequent traveler.

Thankfully, the writings of the apostle Paul provided the encouragement for being an on-the-go prayer when he wrote, "Pray without ceasing" (1 Thessalonians 5:17). The first time I heard this exhortation was in a sermon my dad preached when I was a young teen. I remember at that time thinking how odd the idea sounded. I wondered if it meant we were supposed to walk around on our knees while praying out loud. If so, all the Christians I knew were being terribly disobedient. But, of course, in time I learned that's not what Paul intended.

Contained in the word "pray" are the actions of confessing, submitting, petitioning, praising, and giving thanks. "Without ceasing" refers to being *constantly* in prayer, not in a perpetual action of kneeling, and bowing, and praying. Basically, Paul taught the people to have and maintain an *attitude* of prayer.

Taking my cue from Paul's instruction, I approached my Wednesday of prayer and fasting feeling confident in knowing that I could pray inwardly no matter what I was doing outwardly...and I could do it at all times. It didn't matter if I was driving a car on the highway or a driving a nail in a board with a hammer, walking through an office building or running through an airport, I could be in prayer deep in my heart as I continued through my day. It was a revelation that at least doubled the amount of praying I did on those days.

The Key to Making the Most of Prayer

In another letter written to the believers in Ephesus, Paul said, "Pray at all times in the Spirit" (Ephesians 6:18). This wasn't about maintaining an attitude of ongoing prayer, as was his instructions to the Thessalonians. Instead, it was about how to *keep a level of effectiveness* in the prayers that were offered.

Paul's challenge was especially important to me because most of my praying on Wednesdays were short prayers woven into the tapestry of my busy life. For those momentary prayers to have maximum effectiveness, I needed to follow Paul's wisdom. Essentially, what he was saying was that anytime I prayed I needed to make sure my prayers were in line with the Spirit of God, His written Word, and His will. Basically, Paul was advising that in order for any of us to "pray in sync" at all times with the Spirit, it was imperative that we be "*filled* with the Spirit" (Ephesians 5:18). And as His redeemed followers, to experience the filling of the Spirit we need to be careful to be submissive to Him, obey His Word, and lean on His guidance.

I wish I could report that I never failed to pray that way, but I had plenty of times when I struggled and failed to be in a consistent and close fellowship with the Lord. That shortcoming made it harder to pray with confidence. However, that's when I knew I could really lean on His grace that was always more than sufficient to forgive my deficiencies. In those times when I felt like a miserable failure, I returned to another one of Paul's encouragements:

> I implored the Lord three times that [the thorn] might leave me. And He has said to me, "My grace is sufficient for you, for power is perfected in weakness." Most gladly, therefore, I will rather boast about my weaknesses, so that the power of Christ may dwell in me.

On more than one Wednesday (and the other days of the week, for that matter), I lifted the awareness of my weaknesses up to the Lord. I still do. Sometimes I do this in a symbolic way. I form my right hand into the shape of a cup, and as I raise it to Him I say, "Here's my cup of weakness, Lord. I'm trusting You to fill it with your power."

How grateful I am that He was and is still faithful to His promise to use my weakness as a container for His strength. Not only does His Holy Spirit come alongside me to restore the joy that comes with fellowshipping with Him, He is also willing to provide prayer support when my weaknesses leave me lost for words to pray:

> In the same way the Spirit also helps our weakness; for we do not know how to pray as we should, but the

Spirit Himself intercedes for us with groanings too deep for words; and He who searches the hearts knows what the mind of the Spirit is, because He intercedes for the saints according to the will of God (Romans 8:26-27).

Fragmented but Forceful

My hope is that you'll always remember that:

- you can pray anytime night or day
- to pray without ceasing is to live with an ongoing "attitude of prayer"
- praying in the Spirit requires living in the Spirit

As you strive to keep these truths in mind, I can tell you from experience that there will be times when your praying will seem fragmented and insignificant. But from the vantage point of standing on a mountain of Wednesdays, I can offer the assurance that your efforts—no matter how frail they seem—will not go unseen or unheard by your Father in heaven. And you can also be encouraged to know that during those stretches of time when you might feel weak or even unable to verbalize a prayer, the fasting you are doing will fill in some of the gaps.

So don't give up making the sacrifices. Those bumps of hunger you'll feel serve to let God know that while your tongue may be silent at the moment, your heart is crying loudly on behalf of the needs of your children.

12

What to Pray

Do not be anxious about anything, but in every situation, by prayer and petition, with thanksgiving, present your requests to God. And the peace of God, which transcends all understanding, will guard your hearts and your minds in Christ Jesus (Philippians 4:6-7 NIV).

When I began devoting one day a week to praying specifically for my children, I not only had questions about *when to pray*, I also wondered about *what to pray*. You too may ask this question, and I'm hopeful the suggestions I offer will be useful for you.

Keep in mind that the following explanation of the approach I took (and still take) to praying is my personal story. I'm not implying this is the only way to pray. I offer it to you as a proposed guideline, especially if you're in the beginning stages of establishing a weekly time of prayer.

How Do I Begin?

Many years ago, during a Sunday-morning sermon, our pastor talked about approaching God in prayer. With the goal of helping us understand the importance of "rightly entering in" to the presence of the Lord, he took us to Psalm 100:4 NIV:

Enter his gates with thanksgiving and his courts with praise, give thanks to him and praise his name. For the

Lord is good and his love endures forever; his faithfulness continues through all generations.

After reading the passage, our pastor pointed out that for mankind the "gate" that opens to the Father in heaven is none other than Jesus Christ—and only Him. That truth is found in John 10:7-9 NIV:

> Jesus said again, "Very truly I tell you, I am the gate for the sheep. All who have come before me are thieves and robbers, but the sheep have not listened to them. I am the gate; whoever enters through me will be saved. They will come in and go out, and find pasture."

Then our pastor reminded us that while the "gate" was a narrow entrance ("enter through the narrow gate," Matthew 7:13), the "courts" was a reference to both the openness of the presence of God and the safety for the saints that is found within the hedges of His protection. Within the environment of God's presence is unending freedom to praise Him.

That Sunday morning the way I prayed was permanently transformed. From then on, nearly every time I've prayed I've started with words of thanks to God for as many of His blessings that I can think of at the time. I say thanks for His provision of food and shelter, a functioning body, the blessing of family and friends. I thank Him for the strength to complete a job I was asked to do. The number of things to be grateful for are endless!

The amount of time you spend in thanksgiving is up to you. The important thing is to do it joyfully each time and never with a hurried, "gotta get this done" attitude. To avoid that mistake, I keep in mind what an incredible privilege it is to go before Almighty God in prayer. To help me remember this fact, I often sing the words to the old song "What a Friend We Have in Jesus." I recommend it to you. Here's the first stanza:

What a friend we have in Jesus,
  all our sins and griefs to bear!
What a privilege to carry everything to God in prayer
O what peace we often forfeit,
  O what needless pain we bear,
All because we do not carry
  everything to God in prayer.[7]

After a time of thanksgiving, I offer praise to God—not for what He's done, but simply for who He is. A great place to start is to read or quote Psalm 18:1-3 NIV:

> I love you, LORD, my strength. The LORD is my rock, my fortress and my deliverer; my God is my rock, in whom I take refuge, my shield and the horn of my salvation, my stronghold. I called to the LORD, who is worthy of praise, and I have been saved from my enemies.

Another option I enjoy, especially when I'm alone in a room or in a vehicle, is to sing praises to the Lord. For example, Psalm 59:17 NIV is a very singable verse and is adaptable to almost any melody you want to give it: "You are my strength, I sing praise to you; you, God, are my fortress, my God on whom I can rely."

Another verse that is short in length but long on praise that can be sung easily is the New King James Version of Psalm 103:1: "Bless the LORD, O my soul; and all that is within me, bless His holy name!" If you don't like to sing, you might memorize the verses I've noted and quote them as you enter God's presence. You can add others as you go along.

As I verbally thank God for His goodness and declare who He is either in word, or song, or both, I trust by faith that God accepts my offerings and will hear my prayer that I am about to offer for my children. At that point, I begin to pray for them specifically.

What Areas of Their Lives Should I Address in Prayer?

Obviously, there are an endless number of specific things to pray about when it comes to children. Health, safety, family relationships, friendships, schooling, and their future are just a few. How these and the other areas of life will apply to your children is something only you know as their parent or grandparent. Because the possibilities for things to pray about are so numerous, I recommend doing the two things I've done that helped keep my focus as I prayed for my children.

1. *Ask your kids, "Is there something I can pray about for you?"* If they give you a prayer request, let them know you'll include it in your time of prayer for them. From experience, I can tell you that their prayer requests will be age appropriate. The very young ones might mention anything from a concern they have for a sick pet to asking for prayer for a friend at Sunday school. Teens might mention a need for God's help with a driver's test or for courage to ask someone out for a date. And if they're in college and your day of prayer for them is on Wednesday, they might call on Tuesday, like my son did, and say, "Dad, if you're doing that 'Wednesday thing' tomorrow, I have a huge test that I really need to pass. Please add it to your list." Whatever their request might be, take it seriously and include it in your prayers.

2. *Meditate on the greatest desires you have for your children that you know God alone can grant.* Write them down and keep the list for referring to when you pray. Update the list occasionally. Doing this is how I eventually wrote the lyric to "Wednesday's Prayer."

Is It Okay to Pray the Same Things Every Week?

As I progressed through the first year of praying each Wednesday specifically for my kids, I realized that a list was developing that included the things I wanted most for God to do for and through my son and daughter. Each week I restated those desires. After several consecutive Wednesdays of covering the same ground, a question came to me about my "regular" prayer that I felt compelled to ask the Lord: "Is it okay to pray the same things every week?"

I won't forget where I was when this question came to mind. I was sitting in a deer stand up in a tree. It was Wednesday morning, about nine o'clock. The fast I was doing had been underway since after supper the evening before, and a hunger pang hit me that made me feel like I could eat the bark off of the tree I was sitting in. The sting of hunger served its purpose—reminding me that it was time to pray.

After a time of thanks and praise, I once again went down the list of things I desired in regard to my kids. Suddenly it occurred to me that maybe my repetitiveness with my prayers might not be a good thing. I stopped mid-prayer and said to God, "Am I bothering You with these repeated requests? If so, I apologize—but You know these are things I really do want for my kids."

I went silent for a few moments, and then I sensed way down in my heart that God had responded to my question. It wasn't anything spooky, weird, or Twilight Zone-ish. Instead, what I heard in my heart was a very soft and tender, "I'm not bothered by that." I've had a few times in my 60-plus years that I'm convinced I heard directly from heaven, and this is one of them. Nothing more needed to be said.

I sat in my treestand feeling immense joy and assurance in my heart that it was perfectly fine with God that I bring the same petition to Him each week. After all, I also had biblical ground to stand on based on the story mentioned in chapter 4, "What Is Effective Praying?" That story is about the widow who persistently bothered the king about a legal matter. The king finally helped her since he knew she wasn't going to stop asking (Luke 18:1-8). Also, I remembered Abraham respectfully returning to God multiple times as he sought to save Sodom and Gomorrah from destruction (Genesis 18).

I went on with my prayer list that morning in the deer stand. After I covered all the areas, I said, "In Jesus' name I pray. Amen." That's when it dawned on me that it would be a good thing to form my list into a song lyric that could be used to assist other parents who wanted some guidance about praying for their children. That morning the song "Wednesday's Prayer" was birthed (see the beginning of this book).

A Good Framework for Praying for Your Children

If the question of what to pray for your children is on your heart like it is on mine, I'd like to suggest a general outline you can choose to follow. Using the "Wednesday's Prayer" lyric, I'll walk you through some thoughts I used to help me stay consistent and focused when I approached God on behalf of my children.

In brief chapters, let's go through the verses line-by-line to garner some insights into praying for our children. Feel free to copy "Wednesday's Prayer" and enlist the words and thoughts for your prayers for your children. I'd be honored if you do.

I've also included a short prayer at the end of each chapter that you can use or draw from for your prayer times.

13

"Father God, to You I Come"

> You have not received a spirit of slavery leading to fear
> again, but you have received a spirit of adoption as
> sons by which we cry out "Abba! Father" (Romans
> 8:15).

Addressing God using the term "Father" carries implications that
are very precious to believers who have put their faith in Him
through His Son, Jesus Christ. The family connection is so strong
that, according to Romans 8:15, as His adopted children we can
even call Him "Abba! Father." The word "Abba" was a tender and
intimate term used by children in biblical days in the way that children today would use "Papa" or "Daddy." An adult child would
use *Abba* as a term of deep and abiding respect for his or her father.
As believers in God, our usage of the word with both of these
implications richly expresses our understanding of the value of our
relationship with God.

In one sense, we are acknowledging that we're completely
dependent on Him like little children. And like children, we freely
go to Him as our daddy. At the same time, we're recognizing that
we should go to Him with an attitude of immense respect and
honor that is due the Being who is not only our heavenly Father
but also the awesome and sovereign God of creation.

There are at least two other scriptures that assure those who
belong to God that He approves of us referring to Him with such
an endearing term.

When Jesus taught His disciples to pray, He instructed them to say, "Our Father *who is in heaven*" (Matthew 6:9). By using the term "our Father," Jesus was including the disciples, and all others who would become His followers, in the family of God.

Jesus told Mary Magdalene, "I ascend to My Father and your *Father, and My God and* your *God"* (John 20:17). After His resurrection from the dead, Jesus met Mary Magdalene, who was standing outside His tomb looking in. The description in John 20:15-18 of what took place during their meeting contains another reason all of us can be confident that we can refer to God as "our Father":

> Jesus said to her, "Woman, why are you weeping? Whom are you seeking?"
>
> Supposing Him to be the gardener, she said to Him, "Sir, if you have carried Him away, tell me where you have laid Him, and I will take Him away."
>
> Jesus said to her, "Mary!"
>
> She turned and said to Him in Hebrew, "Rabboni!" (which means, Teacher).
>
> Jesus said to her, "Stop clinging to Me, for I have not yet ascended to the Father; but go to My brethren and say to them, 'I ascend to My Father and *your* Father, and My God and *your* God.'"
>
> Mary Magdalene came announcing to the disciples, "I have seen the Lord," and that He had said these things to her.

Blessed be the name of the Lord for the eternal blessing of being privileged to say, "Father God, to You I come!" when we approach Him with our concerns for our children.

Prayer

Thank You, O God and Maker of this vast universe, that You have adopted me and made me one of Your own. What great love You've shown me by allowing me to call You Father. I recognize that as Your child I can come to You at any time, just as my children can come to me whenever they want. I approach You with a deep, abiding respect for the awesome God You are.

Right now, with childlike excitement and grown-up respect, I come to You in prayer on behalf of my children. There is no one else I can or want to go to about them because I know that You alone created them and love them the most. In Your Son's name, I pray. Amen.

> Even if there are so-called gods whether in heaven or on earth, as indeed there are many gods and many lords, yet for us there is but one God, the Father, from whom are all things and we exist for Him; and one Lord, Jesus Christ, by whom are all things, and we exist through Him (1 Corinthians 8:5-6).

14

"In the Name of Your Son"

Jesus said to [Thomas], "I am the way, and the truth, and the life; no one comes to the Father but through Me" (John 14:6).

Since we have confidence to enter the holy place by the blood of Jesus, by a new and living way which He inaugurated for us through the veil, that is, His flesh, and since we have a great priest over the house of God, let us draw near with a sincere heart in full assurance of faith, having our hearts sprinkled clean from an evil conscience and our bodies washed with pure water (Hebrews 10:19-22).

To address as "Father" the One who created the universe, the One who is all-knowing, all-powerful, completely holy, entirely righteous, and utterly blameless in every way imaginable is a privilege that should never be taken lightly. It was granted to us by the willing sacrifice that Jesus Christ, God's righteous Son, made on the cruel cross of Calvary, where He willingly allowed Himself to be crucified to atone for all people who have sinned, which is all of us. As a result, we not only have access to God through Christ, but we can also enter His presence with joy and the assurance that our heavenly Father accepts all of us who have placed our trust in Jesus.

May God be praised for providing the way for us to go confidently into His comforting presence to offer Him our sincere thanks for His goodness and majesty, as well as bring to Him the burdens we carry in regard to our children.

PRAYER

Thank You, Jesus, for coming to Earth and becoming the way to the Father. I agree that You alone are the door through which I can approach God. And it's in Your name alone that I can ask for anything in accordance with Your will. Blessed be Your holy name!

[Jesus said,] "If you ask Me anything in My name, I will do it" (John 14:14).

15

"I Bring My Children to Your Throne"

> [Hannah said,] "For this child I prayed, and the LORD
> has granted me my petition which I asked of Him.
> Therefore I also have lent him to the LORD; as long as
> he lives he shall be lent to the LORD" (1 Samuel 1:27-
> 28 NKJV).

Hannah was the mother of Samuel. After she bore this son, her husband, Elkanah, along with all of his house, "went up to offer to the LORD the yearly sacrifice and to his vow." Hannah, however, chose not to go, saying to her husband, "Not until the child is weaned; then I will take him, that he may appear before the LORD and remain there forever" (1 Samuel 1:22 NKJV). Her husband agreed, and she stayed and nursed Samuel until he was weaned. Then she took him to the house of the LORD at Shiloh.

Along with many other young parents at the church Annie and I attended, we followed Hannah's example of taking our children to church and dedicating them to the Lord. When they were still babes in our arms, we carried them to the front of the sanctuary and officially committed each of them into God's hands as our pastor prayed over them. It was a solemn moment in our lives as a mom and a dad, and one we have not forgotten. But that dedication wasn't a onetime thing. It still happens each time Wednesday arrives.

Taking our children to the throne of God not only requires deliberate action, but it is also important to understand what is meant by God's throne. Psalm 89:14 provides the insight: "Righteousness and justice are the foundation of Your throne;

lovingkindness and truth go before You." Taking our children to the throne of God is to introduce them to at least four of the greatest provisions God supplies to mankind:

1. *Righteousness:* The work of God through Christ alone that leads us to holiness. "Without holiness no one will see the Lord" (Hebrews 12:14 NIV).

2. *Justice:* The root of mercy and compassion. "Administer true justice; show mercy and compassion" (Zechariah 7:9 NIV).

3. *Mercy:* Always wins. "Mercy triumphs over judgment" (James 2:13 NIV). "Blessed are the merciful, for they will be shown mercy" (Matthew 5:7 NIV).

4. *Truth:* The key to spiritual and emotional freedom. "You will know the truth, and the truth will set you free" (John 8:32 NIV).

What a tremendous opportunity we have to take our children to God's throne. Doing so will help lead them to the glorious life we long for them to know:

> How blessed are the people who know the joyful sound! O Lord, they walk in the light of Your countenance. In Your name they rejoice all the day, and by Your righteousness they are exalted. For You are the glory of their strength, and by Your favor our horn is exalted. For our shield belongs to the Lord, and our king to the Holy One of Israel (Psalm 89:15-18).

PRAYER

Heavenly Father, thank You for the blessing of my children. You alone are all–knowing, so You are aware of what they're doing, where they're going, and what decisions they're making. None of these things are hidden from You. Still, I pray that my children will feel Your presence, hear Your voice, and seek Your face. I pray that You will bring godly people into their lives who will remind them of Your unfailing, unconditional love and reinforce the divine purpose You have for them. Please defeat the enemy of their souls. Show my children mercy and draw them by Your Holy Spirit into Your arms. In the name of Your Son I ask these things. Amen.

> Behold, children are a gift of the LORD, the fruit of the womb is a reward. Like arrows in the hand of a warrior, so are the children of one's youth (Psalm 127:3-4).

16

"Father, Hear My Cry"

Hear my prayer, O LORD, and give ear to my cry
(Psalm 39:12).

When my children were very small, there were a few times when
they would be playing outside and something would happen that
would cause them to scream for me to come. When the piercing
sound of their cry could be heard even through the brick walls of
our house, I knew it was time to rush outside to see what was going
on. I was sure the dread I felt as I dashed to the door would take
years off my life.

Many times their wailing was due to nothing more than being
on the losing end of some type of sibling rivalry. However, on more
than one occasion, their cries were caused by bloodshed. I will
never forget the morning I heard Nathan yelling and, when I shot
outside, I saw a huge gash in the muscle just above his knee. We
made a fast trip to the emergency room and he got several stitches.
On another day, I heard Heidi's scream for me and hurried to our
backyard. There I discovered some deep wounds in Heidi's face put
there by a neighbor's pit bull. Off to the emergency room we went.
Needless to say, I had plenty of reasons to never ignore their cries.

There have been many Wednesdays through the years when
I felt like I was crying out to God the way my kids called for me
when they were physically hurt. As the intense reality of knowing
how much they needed His shelter and guidance seemed pain-
fully overwhelming, I called out to Him from the depths of my

soul. How thankful I was and am for the assurance that my cries are always heard.

Because we live in a world that has become so openly sin-crazed and our lives seem to be daily terrorized by those who love to devise evil, the need for God to cover our children with His mighty hand of protection is greater than ever. How blessed we are to be able to call out to Him and to know that even through the brick walls of cultural chaos, He hears our cries.

Prayer

Thank You, O God, for hearing my cry. No one is as loving as You are. In my heart I come to You with a sense of urgency about the spiritual and physical needs of my children. In this hour, while the walls of time still stand, I lift my voice to You that You might give ear to these things I'm about to ask on their behalf.

Father, do protect them in this evil age we live in. Protect their spirits against the deadly deception that Satan offers them through so many sources, including the media and friends who have no concern or concept of holiness. Protect my children's flesh from the dangerous effects of our sin-saturated culture that poisons our land. God, have mercy on my children. Show me what to do as their parent to help guide them through the maze of this world's madness. In the name of Jesus I cry to You. Amen.

> Give ear to my words, O Lord, consider my groaning.
> Heed the sound of my cry for help, my King and my
> God, for to You I pray (Psalm 5:1).

17

"Above All Else, Lord, Save Their Souls"

What will it profit a man if he gains the whole world
and forfeits his soul? (Matthew 16:26).

As I considered what the number one thing would be that I would
ask God to do for my children, I thought of what my parents
wanted most for Him to do for my sister and me. The two of us
grew up in the care of a mom and dad who were committed to following Christ and making sure their children did as well.

One incident that told me in no uncertain terms that the salvation of my soul was the most important thing to my parents
was mentioned in chapter 1 of this book, "The Heritage of Prayer."
To quickly recap, my mother entered my bedroom one morning
when I was a young teen and prayed a heart-stopping prayer I'll
never forget. She told God if I wasn't going to follow Him later
in life, that He should take me to heaven on the spot. No matter
where I went, no matter how far from home I traveled, my mother's tearful prayer followed me and haunted my heart. On more
than one occasion I was in the midst of an opportunity to do something I knew wasn't morally good and thought of her prayer. The
effect of the remembrance helped me make choices I knew would
please God.

Through my years as a dad, whenever Wednesday came around,
I always included this line: "Above all else, Lord, save their souls." I
said these words in the spirit of my mother's approach to her brave
prayer over me. My wish was not for my kids' lives to be cut short,

but that they would know a long life filled with the joy that comes with redemption and loving the Lord.

PRAYER

O Lord God, I offer my thanks to You for providing the way for my children to be redeemed. How great is the love You've shown us through Your Son and His willingness to shed His blood for our sins. I know there isn't a greater need that my children have than for their souls to know the saving grace that is through Your Son, Jesus Christ. May they come quickly to the realization that He alone is their hope for redemption. Draw them to You, God, and to an understanding of this eternal truth through the work of Your Holy Spirit. Have mercy on my children. In Jesus' holy name I pray. Amen.

> [Mary] will bear a Son; and you shall call His name Jesus, for He will save His people from their sins (Matthew 1:21).

18

"Draw Them Near You; Keep Them Close"

Draw near to God and He will draw near to you (James 4:8).

I have drawn you with lovingkindness (Jeremiah 31:3).

Each week when I came to this line in "Wednesday's Prayer," different images came to mind depending on the age of my children. When they were very young, I thought of how I would give them the "come over here" wave and how quickly they responded by running and playfully jumping into my arms or onto my lap. I genuinely wanted them to be close to me, and I enjoyed their eagerness to be there. Seeing the look on their faces that said "I like it here and I feel safe" was a sight I cherished. In the same way they responded to me, I longed for them to respond to their heavenly Father.

As they progressed into adolescence and their early teen years, they grew out of the era of jumping into their daddy's arms, which was good for my back. However, they still wanted to be close. Because I wanted their nearness as well, my call for them to join me changed with the times. I discovered that I could tap in to their interests and hobbies. As a result there were more fishing and hunting excursions, more bicycle rides, and more camping, concerts, and other ways that helped keep us close.

As I would pray for them in this midseason of their lives in our home, I trusted God to use their interests to attract them to

Him. One example of how God answered this prayer involved my son's passion for music. One of the Christian rock groups Nathan enjoyed had a song about running to the safety of God's presence when being attacked by the devil with temptation. Nathan found himself in a situation that presented him with the opportunity to indulge in some visuals he knew wouldn't please the Lord or his parents. In the midst of the trying moment, the echoes of the lyrics to that song about resisting temptation flooded his mind. He literally ran out of the place to escape the temptation. Later he told us that in his heart he ran to Jesus. Hearing the report of how God had drawn our son to His ways through his interest in music was incredibly uplifting.

Today, now that my children are in their adult years, our relationship has shifted to being as much peers as parents. Now that their world is filled with the challenges of raising their own children, I've yet another image when I pray that they will be drawn into God's presence. I see that they obviously enjoy being close to their children, so I often ask God to teach them that in the same way He still desires their closeness.

Why do I want this kind of closeness between God and my kids? The best explanation I can give is found in God's Word:

> Now the Spirit of God came on Azariah the son of Oded, and he went out to meet Asa and said to him, "Listen to me, Asa, and all Judah and Benjamin: the Lord is with you when you are with Him. And if you seek Him, He will let you find Him; but if you forsake Him, He will forsake you" (2 Chronicles 15:1-2).

I pray that my children will always say, "As for me, the nearness of God is my good" (Psalm 73:28).

Prayer

Father, thank You that Your Spirit bears witness with my spirit that my children and I are Your children. How kind of You to seek our fellowship. I pray that my children will develop a deep and lasting longing in their hearts to be near You. I know that is where they'll find safety, joy, and freedom. Blessed be Your Son's name, in which I pray. Amen.

19

"Be the Shield Against Their Foes"

The Lord is my strength and my shield; my heart trusts in Him, and I am helped (Psalm 28:7).

When my children were very young, the fact that they would even need a shield of protection in this life was upsetting to me. As much as I wished it weren't so, I had to face the sobering fact that they had enemies that could harm them physically and spiritually.

Because they were born into a world that has been infected by the spiritual impurity of sin, I was well aware that their physical environment was a dangerous place for them to live (Romans 5:12). As parents, Annie and I did all we could to protect them from the viruses and germs that could invade their bodies and make them sick. For example, when we carried them to the church nursery, we would stop at the door and observe before entering. If we saw runny noses and heard hacking coughs from their would-be playmates, we raised the shield of protection. More than once we wheeled around and headed to the sanctuary with them in our arms in an effort to deflect the "gift" that the ailing toddlers might give to our children.

When it came to their physical well-being, I knew there was a host of other deadly diseases that could attack them that I had no control over. Whenever I saw pictures of kids with baldness due to cancer or heard of children who had serious accidents, such as pulling a boiling pot of water off the stove, I shuddered in dread. Those images and others that represented the many ways life-threatening pain could come to a child were often in my head when I prayed for my kids. I trusted God to know that all calamities were on my list when I said, "Be the shield against their foes."

On a spiritual level, I was well aware that the world my children came to was even more dangerous. Their greatest enemy, the devil, not only wanted to destroy them physically, he also wanted them to be spiritually dead. I realized that when Jesus said, "The thief comes only to steal and kill and destroy," He was talking about the jealous and vicious religious leaders of His day, but it was also applicable to the devil's intent when it comes to all people, including my children (John 10:10).

I knew that my son and daughter were under a constant barrage of attacks from the enemy of their souls. I also knew that to try to name them all each week would be next to impossible. Instead, as I recognized specific attacks I would mention them when I got to this point in my Wednesday prayer. Anger, fear, jealousy, lust, haughtiness, and laziness were just a few of the fiery darts the enemy of our souls threw at my kids. In addition to these onslaughts, there were the negative influences that came from friends and classmates that the enemy used, not to mention the entertainment opportunities that contained damaging ungodliness. There was much to pray about!

The good news is that the same shield Jesus provided for those who were attacked by the religious wolves he referred to is the same shield that will protect us from our enemies today. Jesus tells us who the shield is: "I am the good shepherd; the good shepherd lays down His life for the sheep" (John 10:11). Jesus is the One I wanted as my children's protection against the enemies of their bodies, souls, and spirits. And nothing has changed. He is still who I have in mind when I pray today. "Jesus, be the shield against their foes..."

PRAYER

O great Defender of my faith, thank You for being the shield against every foe that comes against my children. You alone are able to deflect the flaming arrows of the enemy who seeks to destroy them. I pray that You will continue to be their protector throughout their days. Build their faith in You as their Defender. In Your name I ask this for the sake of their physical and spiritual well-being. Amen.

> Every word of God is tested; He is a shield to those who take refuge in Him (Proverbs 30:5).

20

"Make Them Yours, Not Mine"

The angel of the LORD called to Abraham a second
time from heaven, and said, "By Myself I have sworn,
declares the LORD, because you have done this thing
and have not withheld your son, your only son, indeed
I will greatly bless you" (Genesis 22:15-17).

The well-known account of Abraham's willingness to sacrifice his
son Isaac in obedience to God has been an ongoing challenge to
me regarding my children. This story often came to mind whenever it was time to pray for them. Even though I knew that God
provided Abraham a replacement sacrifice in the form of a ram
that "just happened" to be caught in a nearby thicket, it was still a
little nerve-testing to say to God, "Make my kids Yours, not mine."
But I knew to be unwilling to release them to the Lord would not
please Him who sent them (and the joy that came with them) into
my life.

In addition to the Abraham/Isaac story, there's another inspiring account of someone presenting someone they loved to the
Lord that was of great value:

Three of the thirty chief men went down to the rock
to David, into the cave of Adullam, while the army of
the Philistines was camping in the valley of Rephaim.
David was then in the stronghold, while the garrison
of the Philistines was then in Bethlehem. David had
a craving and said, "Oh that someone would give me

water to drink from the well of Bethlehem, which is by the gate!" So the three broke through the camp of the Philistines and drew water from the well of Bethlehem which was by the gate, and took it and brought it to David; nevertheless David would not drink it, but poured it out to the Lord; and he said, "Be it far from me before my God that I should do this. Shall I drink the blood of these men who went at the risk of their lives? For at the risk of their lives they brought it." Therefore he would not drink it. These things the three mighty men did (1 Chronicles 11:15-19).

When I read that David's respect for the "blood risk" that the three unusually brave men had taken was so deep that he poured the water out to honor the Lord, I saw a picture of what I should do with my children. Because my wife literally risked her life to present my son and my daughter to me, to use them for any selfish purpose whatsoever would be to dishonor my God and her. For that reason, whenever I prayed, "Make them Yours, not mine," I trusted God to know that I was pouring them out to Him and trusting that He would accept them as His own to use in whatever way He chose. This is an attitude I still have in regard to their lives.

Prayer

Thank You, Father, for my children who came to me through my dear wife's hard and dangerous labor. Because of the bloodshed that was required of her to bear them, it would be terribly foolish for me to selfishly consume "the refreshing water" that they are to me. I ask You to accept my children as my gift of gratitude to You for the joy I've known in being a dad. Use them as You wish. They are Yours. In Jesus' name I pray. Amen.

21

"Give Them Peace in Christ Alone"

The peace of God, which surpasses all comprehension,
will guard your hearts and your minds in Christ Jesus
(Philippians 4:7).

Whenever I pray, "Give them peace in Christ alone," my thoughts always go to the words Paul wrote. While in prison, he penned them to the believers who were facing persecution in their small town of Philippi. Though there was opposition from the believers' pagan neighbors, Paul urged the Christ followers to respond to the trouble this way: "Rejoice in the Lord always; again I will say, rejoice! Let your gentle spirit be known to all men. The Lord is near" (Philippians 4:5).

These responses Paul encouraged were totally opposite of the reactions their foes expected of those they were persecuting. I've often wondered if Paul was thinking of David's words: "You prepare a table before me in the presence of my enemies" (Psalm 23:5). Like a gracious host at a banquet who fills the table with all a guest desires, God supplies all the peace we need, *and* He does it even when our enemies are near.

The peace that God provides is the kind I pray my children will experience. I know this peace will come to them only through a loving, personal relationship with Jesus Christ. Whether their enemy at the moment is fear, doubt, confusion, disappointment, sickness, or any other force that wars against them, my prayer is that they'll choose to rest in knowing that they belong to God and He is—and will always be—on their side.

PRAYER

Thank You, Jesus, for standing with those who call on You in faith. I pray that You will show my children that their hearts and minds can rest knowing that You are their "Big Brother" who will not allow their foes to overtake them. May the peace that comes from that blessed knowledge be that which astounds their enemies. And may that peace You give be with my kids all their days. In Your name I pray. Amen.

> Blessed be the God and Father of our Lord Jesus Christ, who according to His great mercy has caused us to be born again to a living hope through the resurrection of Jesus Christ from the dead, to obtain an inheritance which is imperishable and undefiled and will not fade away, reserved in heaven for you, who are protected by the power of God through faith for a salvation ready to be revealed in the last time (1 Peter 1:3-5).

22

"In Their Sorrow, Be Their Song"

The LORD is my strength and song, and He has become
my salvation (Exodus 15:2).

As my children were growing up, the times of sorrow they experienced were always hard to watch. Whether they felt sadness because they received only a yellow participation ribbon for their project in a grade-school science fair or in their teens a friendship was damaged by a horribly unkind remark, their moments of despair were very real to them and to me as well. But as excruciating as these times were, the seasons of sorrow were good training grounds for teaching them that the Lord could bring a song of joy back to their souls if they turned to Him.

One of the most memorable examples of a teachable moment of sorrow that our children experienced took place after an all-day drive to West Virginia to visit their grandparents. Waiting at the farm was a little puppy we had rescued in Nashville a few weeks earlier. We'd taken it there to enjoy the freedom that the open land could provide for an energetic dog. We were all anticipating a sweet reunion with Mark.

I remember how jovial our kids were as we arrived at the farm and drove up the long lane to the house. They could hardly wait for the car doors to open so they could run to find Mark and feel his furry body in their arms again. They greeted their grandmother with hugs, big smiles, and in unison asked, "Where's Mark?"

Annie's mom stood up straight and looked over them at Annie and me with that noticeable, "I don't have good news" look. My heart sank. Then she looked at Nathan and Heidi who were anxiously waiting to know where they could find Mark. With a deep sigh, she said, "I'm so sorry to tell you, kids, that Mark was killed by some very mean dogs yesterday. He's buried in the field behind the barn."

In one moment Heidi and Nathan were giggling in anticipation of hugging Mark and in the next moment their eyes gushed with tears of sadness. Mine did too, as did Annie's. Like pushing the stop button on a CD player, the finger of bad news halted the melody of happiness that had played in all of our hearts.

Though he was "just a dog," Mark was so dear to us that the grief we all felt was huge. For Annie and me it was especially painful to watch our kids feel such intense sorrow. It seemed that the only appropriate thing was to silently whisper the words of a prayer I said on so many Wednesdays: "Lord, in their sorrow, be their song." I had to trust God to reveal to my children that He was aware of their pain and really did care about it and them.

At the moment, the best I could offer the kids was a long, group hug and a time of sharing the sorrow. The wisdom in the old saying, "With friends, joys are doubled and sorrows are halved" held true. Our bearing of each other's burden of sadness while sitting at the picnic table in the Williamsons' front yard helped a lot.

Eventually we were able to talk about the loss of Mark—how we trusted God to help us with the hurt and how leaning on Him in that hour of sorrow was the only thing that helped us feel any joy at all. Thankfully, we did what Psalm 55:22 says: "Cast your burden upon the LORD and He will sustain you."

After that day, often when I prayed "in their sorrow, be their song," I thought of Mark the dog. My hope was that in the future when sorrows of even greater impact gripped my children's hearts, they would remember that in the midst of it Christ alone is the One who can restart the CD player, so to speak, so that the comforting song of His presence will fill them.

Prayer

Thank You, God, that I can cast my cares on You because You care for me. Just knowing that You see even the smallest of causes for the tears that come to the eyes of Your children is a blessing beyond measure. Please help my children know how deeply You care about the burdens of their hearts. Let that awareness bring the melody of hope to their hearts even while they hurt with grief. In Christ's name. Amen.

[The Lord's] song will be with me in the night (Psalm 42:8).

23

"No Other Joy Would Last as Long"

These things I have spoken to you so that My joy may be in you, and that your joy may be made full (John 15:11).

Our family traveled constantly as our children were growing up. Being recording and concert artists, nearly every weekend we piled into our van and headed somewhere. Though almost every mile we traveled as a foursome was for ministry purposes, thankfully none of us resented *getting* there to do it. But *going* there was a different matter. With some discipline and effort, we managed to tolerate the traveling. However, everything was different when the trip was for the purpose of family fun.

Unlike the quiet, wordless, resolved feeling that came with heading out of town to work, when it was a play destination such as a distant lake or amusement park, there was an excited chatter that came from the backseats. The happiness was almost too much for the kids to bear. Even then, Annie and I noticed that the excitement seemed to last only 50 or 60 miles.

Sure enough, though we were off to have fun somewhere, after about an hour the thrill of traveling would start to fade. That's when one of them would ask the inevitable question that all parents in front seats of cars on long trips have heard: "How much longer till we get there?"

One day while heading to Missouri to spend a couple of days at a lake, we'd hardly made it out of the state of Tennessee when I heard "the question." With only about 75 miles behind us and another 300 miles to go, I decided to use the moment to teach them something I hoped they wouldn't forget. I'd tried it before on trips, but wasn't sure my message had gotten through. So once again I attempted to show them the difference between happiness and joy.

"Kids, happiness is the feeling you had when you got into the car this morning. You could hardly sit still as you thought about the jet skis and the hot dogs that are waiting for us in Missouri. Your eyes were bigger than the Frisbees in the trunk of this car. What happened to that happiness?"

The kids just looked at each other as if to say, "We feel a lesson coming on."

All they seemed concerned about was that the miles weren't going by fast enough. I continued. "Happiness is the thrill of setting out on the journey. Joy is in knowing what waits for you when you get there. If you can keep your eyes on that prize, enduring the next 300 miles won't be so tough."

The atmosphere seemed to change in the car. There was a resurgence of chatter in the backseats about swimming, fishing, eating, and so forth. I felt relieved that they seemed to have picked up on the idea that happiness is dependent on what's happening at the moment, while joy is not. Joy is more of a long-term feeling that has more to do with what we *believe* will happen. Happiness is short lived; joy lasts a long time. Happiness depends on our flesh; joy rests in the Holy Spirit. That's what I wanted my kids to know that morning in the car and to remember for the rest of their days.

What I taught my kids about joy was what I often thought about when I prayed this line from "Wednesday's Prayer": "No other joy would last as long." I wanted the Lord to instill in them the reality that sometimes in life the journey would feel long and bumpy because of sorrow, fear, disappointment, or other unwanted trials. I also wanted Him to help them understand that if His presence is their ultimate destination, there would be joy in the journey.

Prayer

Father, how thankful I am that You are my source of lasting joy. You alone are able to reveal to my children the fullness of the joy that knowing You brings. Let them know that even a hundred years full of happy moments here on earth will be no comparison to just one moment in Your presence in heaven. In You there is eternal joy. Nothing else will last as long. Let them see this truth. In Jesus' name I pray. Amen.

> [God] will wipe away every tear from their eyes; and
> there will no longer be any death; there will no longer
> be any mourning, or crying, or pain (Revelation 21:4).

24

"Father, Calm Their Fear"

The LORD is my light and my salvation; whom shall I fear? (Psalm 27:1).

As my children were growing up, I knew it wasn't a matter of *if* they would face fear, it was a matter of *when*. And I knew that when the daunting darkness of terror would engulf them, the only source of comfort would be the light of God's presence. To illustrate how God's light can bring comfort in the face of fear, I can point to what happened during a four-day hike my daughter, Heidi, and I took on the Appalachian Trail (AT) when she was a teenager.

With our backpacks filled with more than enough supplies to last four days, Annie drove us to Virginia to pick up the trail. After exiting the car and swinging the heavy packs onto our backs, we said our goodbyes and stepped out. Within 200 yards we were starting to climb, and the extra weight, along with the sudden steep ascent, tested our muscles in a serious way.

Though the path was long and seemed endlessly straight up, we were having a great time. The early-June weather was perfect, at least until the afternoon of the third day of our trek. Then, as if nature decided we'd had enough fun, the skies darkened, a thick mist rolled in, and the temperature dropped at least 20 degrees.

As the unwelcomed change in the weather was taking place, Heidi and I were ascending the last mountain we needed to cross to get to the place where Annie would pick us up the next evening. To make things even worse, a steady drizzle began to fall. As a result, our pace slowed drastically due to the slick mud on the steep trail.

We didn't want to face the facts, but we knew we wouldn't reach the top of the rain-soaked mountain by sunset as we'd planned.

With just an hour of daylight left, we decided to quickly set up camp and wait there in hopes the foul weather would pass. It didn't. Then night fell on us like a cold blanket. We were stuck in our little tent with no fire, no hot food to enjoy, and a wind that whipped the tent like someone angrily beating a rug on a clothesline with a broom.

The darkness in the tent was blacker than the inside of a closed casket, and it felt as ominous. The sound of the wind that rushed through the trees seemed louder than the roar of a passing train, and it made the night even scarier. Then we both started worrying about one of the big trees being pushed over onto our tent by a vicious gust. There was no sleep to be had.

As we lay in the tomblike tent, I decided to go ahead and turn on a flashlight. I wasn't sure if there was enough battery power to last the rest of the trip, but the darkness was simply too heavy to wait. I dug through the pockets in my backpack for it like a blind man. When I found it, I slid the switch to the on position. I'll not forget how suddenly different our world felt when the light instantly dispelled the darkness.

The look of worry on Heidi's face was still there when the light came on, but within a few seconds her countenance noticeably changed. Her wrinkled brow slowly returned to youthful smoothness, and the tremor in her voice gradually went away. I'm sure I had the same reaction. We spent the hours talking in the yellow glow of the light that bounced off the tent material. Thankfully we made it through the night and greeted the sunrise with grateful hearts for clear skies.

When we look back on those four days on the AT, the night we spent dealing with the harsh elements stands out as the most memorable part of our hike. And I still remember the complete alteration in our attitudes when the tent filled with light. Our worry turned to confidence, our dread was replaced with a certain calm, and our doubt turned to belief that all would be well.

Often when I pray "Father, calm their fear," what Heidi and I experienced that night on a tall mountain in Virginia comes to mind. I long for her and her brother to know the calm that the light of Christ can bring to their hearts. I want them to sense the peace that He provides, especially when the weather turns really bad on the trail of life.

PRAYER

O God of perfect light, thank You for the comfort I can know by allowing You to shine in my life when the world turns dangerously dark. I pray You will fill my children's hearts with the light of Your love and deliver them from the ravages of the storms that will sometimes blacken their days and nights. May You be praised for being the Son who rises in their souls and calms their fears. In Your Son's name, I pray. Amen.

O [God] send out Your light and Your truth, let them lead me (Psalm 43:3).

25

"Guide Their Feet, Lord; Light Their Path"

The steps of a man are established by the LORD, and
He delights in his way (Psalm 37:23).

Your word is a lamp to my feet and a light to my path
(Psalm 119:105).

The longing I had that God would go before my children and
guide them safely through the wilderness of this life was a burden I
carried for them when they were young, and I still carry it. When I
pray "Guide their feet," the image I often return to is an elk-hunting
trip my son, Nathan, and I took to Montana with expert guide
Randy Petrich.

I recall what a picture of faith the hunt was. We were two East-
erners who went West dreaming about the incredible beauty of
Montana, sighting a sizable beast, making an accurate shot, taking
celebratory pictures, and enjoying the tasty bounty. As for knowing where the animals might be and how to get to them, we were
clueless. We desperately needed Randy's knowledge. And if we got
stranded in the backcountry, Randy would be the only one who
knew how to get back to the comfort and safety of camp.

Though these were the facts, Nathan and I still headed west-
ward with big smiles and zero fear because we believed we could
completely trust Randy with our lives and our dreams of success.
In essence, we put our trust in him to "guide our feet."

I'm happy to report that our five-day hunt with our well-skilled guide yielded a six-by-six bull for each of us. What a thrill it was (for the humans).

Just like Randy competently led us through the gigantic territory of Montana and helped us find what we were looking for, God, who intimately knows the vastness of the physical and spiritual world we live in, is able to lead all of us safely through it. He's the *only* One I want as a permanent Guide for my children. I know He will lead them to the one thing they desperately need—a personal relationship with Him.

> The mind of man plans his way, but the Lord directs
> his steps (Proverbs 16:9).

PRAYER

God, I thank You that You are graciously willing and fully able to lead my children through this world that can be quite a spiritual, emotional, and moral wilderness. I pray that You will teach them to trust You in their days as well as their nights as they follow You. I ask You to give them an understanding of the value of Your Word and how You use it to light the steps You've ordered for them. In Christ's name I ask this. Amen.

> My son, observe the commandment of your father and
> do not forsake the teaching of your mother; bind them
> continually on your heart; tie them around your neck.
> When you walk about, they will guide you; when you
> sleep, they will watch over you; and when you awake,
> they will talk to you. For the commandment is a lamp
> and the teaching is light; and reproofs for discipline
> are the way of life (Proverbs 6:20-23).

26

"May Their Eyes on You Be Cast"

Let us run with endurance the race that is set before us, fixing our eyes on Jesus, the author and perfecter of faith (Hebrews 12:1-2).

"May their eyes on You be cast" was my prayerful paraphrase of Hebrews 12:2. When I prayed for my son and daughter using this line, I did so with a mixture of great hope and intense concern. I was hopeful that the "eyes of their hearts" would be firmly focused on Christ and His teachings in His Word. If they were, according to the promise in Scripture, Jesus would not only create faith in them, but He would also complete (mature) their faith. The result would be that they would find strength for successfully running the race of life.

I was deeply concerned because of what was included in verse 1 of Hebrews 12: "Let us also lay aside every encumbrance and the sin which so easily entangles us." I was well aware that if they fixed their physical eyes on the pleasures of sin, they would grow weary and lose heart (verse 3). They wouldn't be able to run the race with endurance.

I hoped my children's eyes would be fixed on Christ alone, and that they would understand that as they looked to the Lord with hearts that were fully committed to Him, He was looking for them, as promised in 2 Chronicles 16:9: "The eyes of the LORD move to and fro throughout the earth that He may strongly support those whose heart is completely His."

I can think of no greater joy than to know that my children

walk in God's truth and that because of it, His eyes will be cast on them. To realize that the God of this entire universe has my kids in His sight is a great comfort.

PRAYER

Thank You, O God, that You see my children. Bless You for being the Creator and the Completer of their faith. I pray they will keep the eyes of their hearts fixed on You just as they would fix the eyes of their flesh on a prize they desperately long to have. When they come to a crossroad in life, may they see only the cross of Christ and the hope found in Him. And, Father, I pray against the onslaught of the enemy of their souls who tries to entice them to look away from You. I trust You to be the winner in the battle for my children's attention. To Your glory and for the sake of their spiritual, physical, and emotional well-being, I pray this in Jesus' name. Amen.

> My eyes are continually toward the LORD, for He will pluck my feet out of the net (Psalm 25:15).

27

"Give Their Hands a Kingdom Task, a Purpose for Their Years"

> [Jesus said,] "I glorified You on the earth, having accomplished the work which You have given Me to do" (John 17:4).

Our children were just about to leave adolescence when I started fasting and praying each Wednesday for them. They were immersed in learning math, English, American history, and other academic requirements that came with school. What their future held in terms of vocation was totally unknown. That didn't mean, however, that training was to be ignored. What their hands would find to do was important to me.

One of the reasons I cared so deeply about what they would do with their energy and time was because of what Jesus included when talking to God: "the work which You have given Me to do." I made the assumption that God prescribes jobs for people. I prayed about what that work would be for my kids because they belonged to the Lord. He would give them something to do that would promote His kingdom on the Earth.

I didn't pray specifics though. I didn't say, "Lord, send them to a mission field or call them to minister to a congregation." I didn't ask Him to make them Sunday school teachers or leaders of charitable organizations. Instead, my prayer was intentionally general because I wanted *God to choose the work* they would do.

Now that my kids are grown and on their own, folks have asked Annie and me from time to time what they ended up doing with their lives. Some are surprised when they hear that they aren't in some type of formal, church-related ministry. We've heard them say, "Wow, I thought they'd be a pastor or pastor's spouse, maybe a worship leader, or in some capacity of leadership in a church setting...or even a missionary." When some learn our children fill none of the roles they think of as "being in the ministry," they react as though our children aren't doing God's work. We respond by biting our tongues and holding back our righteous indignation. Then we typically say,

> They *are* in ministry. They're devoted spouses to their mates and are raising their children in the admonition of the Lord. They have unique callings from the Lord. As a skilled, award-winning music producer and songwriter, our son speaks words of life and hope to those in the music world who ask about his faith. Our daughter, besides being a supportive wife to a man who is a CFO at a national company, schools their three girls, encourages her friends spiritually, and is an artist who donates her interior designer skills at their church.

God answered our prayers to "give their hands a kingdom task, a purpose for their years." We continue to pray He'll bless them with work that glorifies Him.

Prayer

Lord, thank You for the work You call my children to perform. Make it clear to their hearts and minds what they are to do, and give them the strength to do it. Bless them with a double portion of knowledge and insight as they learn how to do the work You assign. May they always work in ways that bring glory to You. In Your name I pray. Amen.

28

"As My Flesh Cries Out for Bread, May I Hunger, Lord, Instead"

[Jesus said,] "Is not life more than food?" (Matthew 6:25).

For someone who loves to eat, the idea of fasting isn't all that welcome. When Tuesdays came and I remembered that the next day would be a day of fasting, my flesh would begin to whine like an unhappy child. I discovered that it wasn't a matter of *if* the body would cry out against being intentionally deprived of food, it's *how loud* it will cry out.

In order to follow through with the Wednesday prayer plan, I had to face the protest that my "natural man" made against not eating and, instead, focus on my spiritual desires. Quite honestly, it was an intense challenge. The way I fought back was to ask the Lord to replace my hunger for food for my flesh with something that would be spiritually nourishing for my children—which was, and still is, the Word of God.

> I discipline my body and make it my slave (1 Corinthians 9:27).

PRAYER

Thank You, Father, for the opportunity to fast so You'll know how serious I am about praying for my children. I ask You for Your strength to be faithful to this cause and trust that You'll bless my efforts. In Your Son's righteous and holy name. Amen.

29

"[I Pray] That My Children Would Be Fed on Your Words of Life"

How sweet are Your words to my taste! Yes, sweeter than honey to my mouth! (Psalm 119:103).

There's a scene in an old episode of *The Andy Griffith Show* where skinny Deputy Sheriff Barney Fife sits down at the local diner and orders breakfast. He says something like, "I don't want much this morning. Just give me some orange juice, a bowl of cereal, a stack of wheats, three eggs over easy, bacon on the crisp side, white toast with butter, and coffee." The waitress stops writing, presses her little order book against her chest and smiles very sweetly at her hungry customer. Then, with a motherly tone in her voice, she says, "Oh, it does my heart good to see a thin man eat!"

Whenever Annie prepared a meal and watched our children consume it, I saw a smile on her face that resembled the look of pleasure on the face of Barney's waitress. Annie and I loved knowing our children were well fed. In the same way that we wanted our kids to get the benefit of food for their growing bodies, we wanted their "spiritual bodies" to be well fed. We were well aware that the best source of body-building nutrition for their souls was, and still is, the Word of God. For that reason, we provided sustenance for their spirits from the Scriptures as often as possible. Our goal was to make sure they heard some of God's Word every day.

With that in mind, we did several things. When they were very young, we read Bible-based storybooks with them and took them to church so they would hear biblical truths. When they were a little older, we purchased a One-Year Bible and, as a family, used it as faithfully as possible. When we missed a day, we always made it up. By the end of the year, we all were delighted to have completed reading the entire Bible!

As they entered their teens, we encouraged Nathan and Heidi to be devoted to consuming at least a few verses each day. They were faithful to do so, and today I'm grateful to report that they consider God's Word their most important resource for guidance in life. The only thing more gratifying for us as parents is seeing them diligently reading and teaching the truths of the Scriptures to their own kids. What a blessing to know that our grandchildren's spirits are being so well fed.

When I asked God to replace my hunger for food with a hunger that my children would be fed on His Word, He was gracious in answering that prayer. I hope you'll trust Him to do the same for you.

PRAYER

Thank You, God, that You've provided Your written Word that will feed the need my children have for truth. I ask You to help me as a parent and grandparent to do all I can to create a hunger in their hearts for Your Word. I want them to have an appetite that is deep and continuous. I know if they feed on Your Word, their lives will be blessed with spiritual and emotional health and they'll be morally healthy. Even their physical bodies will benefit from the spiritual nourishment Your Word offers. In Christ's name, I bless You for meeting these needs. Amen.

> [Jesus said,] "Blessed are those who hunger and thirst for righteousness, for they shall be satisfied" (Matthew 5:6).

30

What to Do Thursday to Tuesday

Through the years since my friend and I started our "Wednesday's Prayer," that particular day generated a mixture of feelings. On one hand, my mind and flesh dreaded Wednesdays because I knew I would wake up in the morning and walk past the pantry where the Cheerios box was stashed. There'd be no sound of the crisp, little "O's" falling into a glass bowl, no sliced banana with them, no whole milk to drown the combination, no wheat toast to slather with butter and strawberry jam, and no coffee with real cream. Instead, all I would take as I headed off into the day would be a glass of water and a gulp of fresh air. Wednesday was the day when all the fun for my taste buds was suspended.

On the other hand, my spirit knew that Wednesday was the time when another day had come for me to dig in and talk seriously to God about my children and my friend's daughter, including their spiritual and physical welfare, their futures, their places in this world, and their eventual place in eternity. Yes, sometimes it would take a few minutes to get over the pain that came with ignoring the breakfast, but once I got past it and set my focus on what an incredible opportunity it was to sacrificially pray for young ones I loved and cared about, the hunger for the good that could come to them took over.

At the end of the day when my fast was broken, another mixture of feelings would come. On one hand, my mind and flesh would be so ready to eat that they didn't care what we were having for dinner. I just wanted a lot of it. As far as I was concerned, I would have been happy if Annie would have just salted the tablecloth and served it. And yet my spirit felt a certain sadness that another Wednesday would soon be over and the joy of being victorious and faithful to the cause of praying for the children would fade into the night. But sadness wasn't the only emotion I would feel.

As I ate dinner with my family, deep inside me I would wrestle with guilt over the fact that come the next morning, I would start six days of not being so focused on what I longed for in terms of my children. Each week I faced the same question that came with the completion of another Wednesday: *What can or should I do Thursday to Tuesday?*

I have my mother to thank for providing the help I needed. When I was in my early teens, I recall Mom saying, "Whenever I'm going through the normal course of a day and suddenly someone's name comes to my mind, I don't ignore it. Instead, when it happens I make the assumption that at that moment the person I thought of is in need of prayer. So I pray."

I can't think of a better solution to the Thursday to Tuesday challenge than following my mom's lead. Whispering a prayer for Heidi and Nathan as well as other people whenever I think of them is a wonderful way to fill the focus gap. Does it mean I stop each time I think of them, fall to my knees wherever I am or bow my head and enter into a serious time of prayer? No. Instead, a prayerful response to the thought of someone can be instantaneous, short, and silent. No one else even needs to know that it's happening. The important thing is that I pray for the person.

Several years after I heard Mom say that she secretly prayed for the folks who crossed her mind, I wrote a song that highlights her commitment...

And So They Prayed

A young, golden-haired soldier
Stood in the ranks of the brave
Captain said, "Guns to the shoulder!"
And they quietly marched away

His blues eyes once thrilled his mother
But now they were filled with fear
As he heard the cannons thunder
And the field of the battle drew near

But in that moment far away
A mother whispers, "Amen"
'Cause she thought of her son,
    and so she prayed
Oh, how she prayed for him

His young hands, once they were steady
As he'd hunt by his father's side
But now they trembled as he readied his gun
And the enemy came into sight

But in that moment far away
A father says, "Amen"
'Cause he thought of his son,
    and so he prayed
Oh, how he prayed for him

How swiftly his legs once carried him
As he'd race with his sister to town
But he could not run from the bullet within
And so he fell to the ground

But in that moment far away
A sister says, "Amen"
'Cause she thought of her brother,
    and so she prayed
Oh, how she prayed for him

Well, the letter arrived,
It was stained with blood
    and it was sadly received
And gathering around were the ones he loved
And they began to read

But in that moment far away
A young soldier whispers, "Amen"
'Cause he thought of his family,
    who would hear of his wounds
And so he prayed for them
'Cause he knew they must have been
    praying for him[8]

To all who are praying regularly for children, I urge you to never ignore the thought of them. Let their names and the images of their faces that come to your mind be the call to pray. Whether they're in the next room, playing at a neighbor's house down the street, a thousand miles away at college, on the other side of the world in a military uniform, or somewhere in a city far away tending to their children, when you think of them, quietly lift them up in prayer. As you do, take comfort in knowing that God, who put thoughts of them on your heart, will hear your cry and take care of them as only He can do.

31

Wear the Prayer

Another suggestion that might be helpful in regard to filling the "Thursday to Tuesday" gap as you pray for your children is an idea that has its roots in something my wife did after the terror attack in New York City on September 11, 2001. We'd flown home on the tenth of September, skirting the danger our nation faced, but we were scheduled to fly again not many days later. As we neared the time to travel by air again, the thought of boarding a plane generated a near-debilitating fear in Annie. While she would have much rather not gotten on the flight, she found the courage to do it. How? She didn't go to the airport unprepared. Pinned to the backside of the belt she wore was a piece of paper with these verses from the book of Joshua written on it:

> This book of the law shall not depart from your mouth,
> but you shall meditate on it day and night, so that you
> may be careful to do according to all that is written in
> it; for then you will make your way prosperous, and
> then you will have success. Have I not commanded
> you? Be strong and courageous! Do not tremble or be
> dismayed, for the LORD your God is with you wher-
> ever you go (1:8-9).

In her book *Taking Back Your Life One Thought at a Time*, Annie wrote about using these verses:

> Whenever fear would creep into my heart and the voice
> of dread whispered, I slid my hand under my belt and

touched the words from God I'd written down. When I did that, the enemy would flee and my confidence would return. I used this method countless times on that flight and the many more that followed...

I knew I couldn't eliminate the potential danger nor could I forget what had happened so recently, but I could replace those devastating thoughts and images with the knowledge that nothing can touch me that does not first come through the filter of God's strong and mighty hand.

Taking a cue from Annie's effective and comforting idea of wearing God's Word on her person to help her cope with fear, it would be an equally good idea for parents who are praying for children to "wear the prayer." Carrying a prayer on a piece of paper has no special power; however, it can be an inspiring reminder when you prayerfully think of your children.

If this idea appeals to you, what you carry with you in terms of a prayer is up to you. You can write down your own prayer that states what you want God to do in and through your children or, if the lines in the song "Wednesday's Prayer" represent your desires for your kids, you're welcome to copy the page that has the lyrics on it and wear it in a pocket, wallet, purse, or anywhere else that is easily accessible.

Whatever you decide to do about praying for your children on the six days you're not focusing fully on them, be sure to remember that the enemy of their lives will not be taking a break on those days—but neither will God!

32

Write a Note

I suggest that you write a special note to your children telling them of your plan to pray for them. Believe me, whether they show it or not, they'll be grateful for such a display of your love. Here's a sample note you can choose to use if you're not sure what to write.

> Dear _____,
>
> As your dad, I'm committing to pray and fast for you on Wednesday of each week for the next _____. I love you, and I know our heavenly Father loves you too. Please let me know when you have any specific needs you'd like me to include on that special day when I'm praying specifically for you.
>
> I love you!
>
> From my heart to yours,
>
> Dad

May God richly bless you and your family as you embark on this marvelous journey of dedicated, concentrated prayer for your children.

Your Child Is Not Out of Reach

In light of the fact that the enemy of our souls is so active in capturing and imprisoning those we love, plus the admission that my own past is proof that children are bent toward sinning, you can see why I believe that all of us parents would do well to follow my mom and dad's example by adding fasting to our prayers for our kids. As for my own two children, I want to see them in heaven. For that reason, I desire for the Lord to take me seriously when I take them to His throne in prayer.

Maybe you're seeking the Lord about children who have yet to surrender to Christ or who need to return to the depth of fellowship with Him they once knew. As you pray for them to know His mercy and forgiveness, may God make you mighty in the Holy Spirit and strengthen you as you face the challenges of concentrated prayer and hunger.

Perhaps you're thinking of children teetering on the brink of spiritual oblivion. I encourage you to join the army of those who pray for children. Let God see your hunger for your children's salvation and deliverance by pushing away the food (or the object/ nature of your fast). As you pray, remember these words by David: "Blessed be the LORD, because He has heard the voice of my supplication" (Psalm 28:6). Let the knowledge that God hears your cry be a source of strength for you to continue in prayer.

It might take some time to see results, but don't give up the battle. The physical and emotional energy spent fighting for your kids while here on Earth is no comparison to the unending delight you'll enjoy in eternity because the war was won. No matter how distant your child is from God, there is hope. You can bolster this hope by remembering the story of the widow of Nain.

Jesus was entering the town of Nain when a funeral procession was leaving through the town gate. When He saw the casket and heard the news, Jesus had compassion on the mother. He told her, "Do not weep." Then He touched the coffin, and the bearers came to a halt. Jesus said, "Young man, I say to you, arise!" And the dead man sat up and began to speak. After that, Jesus gave him back to the mother.

What a beautiful picture of what we can do for our sons and daughters who are spiritually dead in their trespasses and sins (Ephesians 1:1-5). We can trust that Christ knows about their condition and that He is willing and able to restore the lives of those who are spiritually dead. And remember, Jesus didn't come to make bad people good. He came to make spiritually dead people alive...including our children. For that reason we must take them to Jesus, for He alone can make them alive again. Please be encouraged. Your child is reachable!

Reachable

There's a boy in his mother's prayers
'Cause lately she's been aware
That he's been drifting too far from the shore
And she's beginning to believe
The boy is getting out of reach
Weary mother, don't you worry anymore

'Cause...
The boy is reachable, I know he's reachable
And to God he's visible, and all things are possible
'Cause if the Lord can reach His hand of love through time
And touch a cold sinner's heart like mine
The boy is reachable...I know he's reachable

There's a girl on her daddy's heart
'Cause lately they've drifted apart
And the company she's keeping
Leads her further away
And he's beginning to believe
The girl is getting out of reach
Oh, weary father, heaven hears you when you pray

'Cause…
The girl is reachable, I know she's reachable
And to God she's visible, and all things are possible
'Cause if the Lord can reach His hand of love through time
And touch a cold sinner's heart like mine
The girl is reachable, I know she's reachable
If this boy is reachable, anyone is reachable[9]

I'm quite certain that my parents didn't think for even a second that I was out of the reach of God's powerful hand of grace. If they were tempted with the thought, I'm sure they considered it the devil's intent to discourage them. One thing that spurred them on to pray without ceasing for me was remembering how God answered the earnest prayers of my Grandmother Chapman as she prayed for her son, who was my Uncle Bud. His story is briefly covered in my book *A Look at Life from a Deer Stand: The Study Guide.* It merits more detail here for the sake of encouraging you if you're feeling disheartened.

Uncle Bud was the eldest of 11 children born to George and Easter Chapman. Uncle Bud was prone to drink, was a constant smoker, and was an avid gambler. He seemed to spend a lot of time at places like the dog race track in the big city 60 miles away. He went with friends, who didn't contribute much to his life in terms of good character.

My Grandma Chapman did not approve of her son's choices

for entertainment, but she could do nothing about it other than pray diligently for him. And that she did until she died in her early eighties. She didn't stay around to see how God would answer her prayers. Instead, she got to see it from heaven's balcony.

Not long before his 74th birthday, Uncle Bud learned he had cancer. Up to that point he'd shown no interest whatsoever in spiritual matters, especially becoming a follower of Jesus Christ. In fact, the people around him didn't dare bring up the subject knowing the ire that he was quick to show at the very mention of it. Even his sweet wife, a longtime believer who had patiently loved her man throughout their married life, couldn't reach him. It took the news of his quickly declining health to get his attention.

Much to the joy of those who loved Uncle Bud, he began to show openness to the encouragement received from his family to trust Christ for his soul's salvation. He was especially attentive to the counsel given to him by my dad (his brother and a preacher). Finally, at the age of 74, he responded to the gospel and committed the rest of his days to Christ.

Family history says that Uncle Bud's conversion was so immediately and vastly transforming that something happened one day that no one could have imagined. During his illness and prior to repentance and accepting the Lord's forgiveness, his friends would come by his house to pick up cash he'd send along for placing bets at the dog races. They'd gamble for him and, if successful, deliver his winnings to him on their way home.

As usual, his friends came by one day to pick up Uncle Bud's stash for betting on the dogs. They discovered things had changed. As they stood around his bed, Uncle Bud announced, "Fellows, I don't gamble anymore. I gave my life to God, and I'm finished with the dogs."

His friends were not only stunned when they heard Bud's words, they also received a witness about Christ's redemptive power. In his last days, Uncle Bud had become an evangelist.

Too weak to go to the local church that had a baptistery, my dad baptized his brother in the bathtub at his house while a few family members and friends stood by singing worship songs. The rejoicing not only happened in Uncle Bud's house—it also happened in heaven as the angels rejoiced with the homecoming of another wayward son. I can't help but think that Easter Chapman, Uncle Bud's mother who had so faithfully petitioned the Lord for her son's salvation, was also praising God for answering her prayers.

I hope you feel more inspired to not give up on going to God on behalf of your children. Perhaps this lyric about Uncle Bud will encourage you as well.

Uncle Bud Came Home

On his way to his final day, Uncle Bud stopped at the cross
Fell on his knees said, "Save me please, Lord. You know
    I'm lost...
Forgive the tears through all the years I've caused in other's
    eyes"
Let the joy bells ring, let the angels sing, and let no one
    criticize

'Cause he's as welcome there as apostle Paul, Matthew,
    Mark, or Luke or John
All that really matters at all, His sins are gone, yes his sins
    are gone
Uncle Bud came home.

Some come home in the morning
Some come home at noon
Some come home when the sun's going down
Uncle Bud came home by the light of the moon[10]

Notes

1. Steve Chapman, "Wednesday's Prayer," Times & Seasons Music, Inc., 1996, BMI. Used by permission. All rights reserved.

2. Steve Chapman, "Mama's Brave Prayer," Times and Seasons Music Inc., 1990, BMI. Used by permission. All rights reserved.

3. Steve Chapman, "Daddy, Dip Your Finger in the Water," Times and Seasons Music, 1996, BMI. Used by permission. All rights reserved.

4. Steve Chapman, "I Want to Go with My Daddy," Times & Seasons Music, 2008, BMI. Used by permission. All rights reserved.

5. Bill Gothard, "Institute of Basic Youth Conflicts," quoted in Ed Skidmore, *A Place at My Father's Table* (Raleigh, NC: lulu.com, 2010), 35.

6. Steve Chapman, Lindsey Williams, Joseph Habedank, "Send Somebody," Times & Seasons Music/Really Big Bison Productions/Habeholt Music, 2013, BMI.

7. Joseph M. Scriven, "What a Friend We Have in Jesus," 1855, Cyber Hymnal, http://www.hymntime.com/tch/, accessed 7/27/15.

8. Steve Chapman, "And So They Prayed," Times & Seasons Music, 1994, BMI. Used by permission. All rights reserved.

9. Steve Chapman, "Reachable," Times & Seasons Music, 1996, BMI. Used by permission. All rights reserved.

10. Steve Chapman, "Uncle Bud Came Home," Times & Seasons Music, 1996, BMI. Used by permission. All rights reserved.

To learn more about Harvest House books and
to read sample chapters, visit our website:

www.harvesthousepublishers.com

HARVEST HOUSE PUBLISHERS
EUGENE, OREGON